Dr. Del's Tier 1

Notes and Exercises

Not Intended for Self-Study

Tutorial Videos for each Lesson are available to expedite the learning.

Craig Hane, Ph.D.
Triad Math, Inc.

Dr. Del's Tier 1 Notes and Exercises

Not Intended for Self-Study

By: Craig Hane, Ph.D.

© 2023 Triad Math, Inc. All Rights Reserved

2023 Edition

Published by:
Triad Math, Inc.
3822 S. Westmont Ave., Bloomington, IN 47403, US
Phone: 01-812-355-3030 ext. 402
Email: info@TriadMathInc.com
www.TriadMathInc.com

Foreword

These are the Notes and Exercises for Dr. Del's Tier 1 Online Math Program for post-elementary students.

The student should be studying these Lessons in a consecutive sequence with the Tutorial Videos and Quizzes.

This book is designed to be used by a student who has access to a good math teacher/tutor or is enrolled in Del's Tier 1 Online Math Program.

You may purchase access to the Dr. Del's Tier 1 Online Math Program Tutorial Videos, if you have not already done so, by emailing info@TriadMathInc.com or by visiting HomeSchoolerToday.com.

Craig Hane, Ph.D., Founder

Tier 1 Notes

TI-30Xa INTRODUCTION

The TI-30Xa Scientific Calculator is very good for Practical Mathematics. We have chosen this model for its ease of use and low cost. You may use another calculator, but be aware that they all have different key positions and work somewhat differently.

This series of lessons will explain the various basic functions and processes we will be using in the Fundamentals Course.

Each lesson will consist of a video explanation of the lesson's topic and homework to reinforce the lesson.

After you have mastered the topic you may take a quiz to prove your mastery of the topic. It is best to master each topic sequentially since later topics may depend on previous topics.

IMPORTANT: Mathematics is like a "contact sport." You must play and practice to master the necessary skills and knowledge.

Most people find mathematics like a game whereby knowledge and skills are acquired over time with practice and study.

Treat it like a game. Have fun! Do not be discouraged by mistakes or setbacks. That is part of the game.

Your learning will be cumulative. You will notice that things that seem difficult today will become easy tomorrow.

1.1 Lessons Abbreviation Key Table

C = Calculator Lesson
P = Pre-algebra Lesson
A = Algebra Lesson
G = Geometry Lesson
T = Trigonometry Lesson

The number following the letter is the Lesson Number.

E = Exercises with Answers: Answers are in brackets [ ].
EA = Exercises Answers: (only used when answers are not on the same page as the exercises.)
ES = Exercises Supplemental: Complete if you feel you need additional problems to work.

1.2 Exercises Introduction

Why do the Exercises?

Mathematics is like a "game." The more you practice and play the game the better you will understand and play it.

The Foundation's Exercises, which accompany each lesson, are designed to reinforce the ideas presented to you in that lesson's video.

It is unlikely you will learn math very well by simply reading about it or listening to Dr. Del, or anyone else, or watching someone else doing it.

You WILL learn math by "doing math."

It is like learning to play a musical instrument, or write a book, or play a sport, or play chess, or cooking.

You will learn by practice.

Repetition is the key to mastery.

You will make mistakes. You will sometimes struggle to master a concept or technique. You may feel frustration sometimes "**WE ALL DO.**"

But, as you learn and do math, you will begin to find pleasure and enjoyment in it as you would in any worthwhile endeavor. Treat it like a sport or game.

These exercises are the KEY to your SUCCESS!

ENJOY!

C1 LESSON: ON/OFF   FIX   DEG   M1   M2   M3

TI-30Xa is the "Power Tool" we will be using.

Keys will be underlined. There are 40 Keys.

36 of these Keys have a dual function indicated in yellow above the key, and reached by the Yellow 2nd Key

On/C is the On and Clear Key: Upper Right

OFF is the Off Key: Row 1 Column 5

In the Display at top of calculator:

M1 M2 M3 are the memory indicators (top left - Lesson C5)

DEG is angle indicator (Lesson C12)

FIX indicates you have fixed the number of digits that appear after the decimal point. It is located above the decimal point at bottom.

Nine digits is the default when you turn on the calculator.

A good practice is to turn the calculator OFF between calculations. Numbers stored in Memory, M1, M2, M3 will not be lost.

Take the C1 Quiz when you are ready.

ON/OFF FIX DEG M1 M2 M3

1. TI-30Xa is a P _ _ _ _ T _ _ _ of math?

2. The TI-30Xa has how many keys?

3. How many of these keys are dual function?

4. You activate a dual function with which key?

5. The ON/C key does what?

6. Where is the ON/C key?

7. Where is the OFF key?

8. How many Memory registers are there in the TI-30Xa?

9. Where is their indicator in the Display?

10. What does the DEG indicate in the display?

11. Where is the FIX function, and what does it do?

12. How do you display "n" digits after the decimal point?

Answers are on C1EA, page 9.

ON/OFF FIX DEG M1 M2   Answers: [ ]'s

1. TI-30Xa is a P _ _ _ _ T _ _ _ of math?   [**Power Tool**]

2. The TI-30Xa has how many keys?   [**40**]

3. How many of these keys are dual function?   [**36**]

4. You activate a dual function with which key?
                    [**Yellow "2ND" Key in upper left corner.**]

5. The ON/C key does what?
          [**Turns TI-30Xa on and Clears the registers, and sets DEG. It does not change memory.**]

6. Where is the ON/C key?   [**Upper Right Corner**]

7. Where is the OFF key?   [**Below the ON/C Key**]

8. How many Memory registers are there in the TI-30Xa?
                          [**Three, M1, M2, M3**]

9. Where is their indicator in the Display?   [**Upper Left**]

10. What does the DEG indicate in the display?
                      [**Angles will be entered in degrees**]

11. Where is the FIX function, and what does it do?

        [**Above the decimal point at bottom. It fixes the number of digits displayed after the decimal point.**]

12. How do you display n digits after the decimal point? [**2nd FIX n**]

We assume you know basic arithmetic operations and rules. If not, you will need some more basic training.

Key k is indicated by **k** the underline.

The = Key is used to complete a calculation.

Addition + Key adds two numbers 3 + 4 = 7

Subtraction - Key subtracts numbers 7 - 2 = 5

Negative numbers will be discussed in Lesson 3

The TI-30Xa will take care of decimal locations.

$$12.3 + 7.5 = 19.8 \qquad 12.3 + 7.05 = 19.35$$

Practice makes perfect!

The calculator is also a very good tool to help you learn the addition or multiplication tables.

And also, to help you learn to do approximate calculations which are a good idea to do a "quick check" for mistakes.

The more you "play" with it…the better you'll get!

ADD + SUBTRACT - EQUAL =

1. What key completes a calculation?

2. Which key adds two numbers?

3. Which key subtracts two numbers?

4. 12.3 + 4.8 = ?

5. 375 + 897 = ?

6. 0.075 + 0.0345 = ?

7. 87 - 39 = ?

8. 12.34 - 7.05 = ?

9. 0.0087 - 0.00032 = ?

10. 12 + 56 + 32 + 89 = ?

11. 37 - 48 = ?

12. 3,879 + 7,425 = ?

13. 2.32 + 0.073 = ?

ADD + SUBTRACT - EQUAL = Answers: [ ]'s

1. What key completes a calculation?   [=]

2. Which key adds two numbers?   [+]

3. Which key subtracts two numbers?   [-]

4. 12.3 + 4.8 = ?   [17.1]

5. 375 + 897 = ?   [1,272]

6. 0.075 + 0.0345 = ?   [0.1095]

7.   87 - 39 = ?   [48]

8. 12.34 - 7.05 = ?   [5.29]

9. 0.0087 - 0.00032 = ?   [0.00838]

10. 12 + 56 + 32 + 89 = ?   [189]

11. 37 - 48 = ?   [-11] (See C3 for Negative Numbers)
12. 3,879 + 7,425 = ?   [11,304] (You supply commas)
13. 2.32 + 0.073 = ?   [2.393]

**Take the C2 Quiz if you are ready,
or do some more exercises, C2ES.**

ADD +   SUBTRACT -   EQUAL =

1. $17.3 + 234.8 + 3.7 = ?$

2. $37.5 + 8.97 = ?$

3. $0.175 + 0.0385 = ?$

4. $97 - 19 = ?$

5. $12.74 - 9.05 = ?$

6. $0.087 - 0.032 = ?$

7. $12 + 96 + 52 + 29 = ?$

8. $57 - 98 = ?$

9. $3,979 + 4,425 = ?$

10. $28 - 12 - 17 = ?$

11. $2.72 + 0.773 = ?$

12. $54,321 - 12,345 = ?$

13. $9,999 - 7,654 = ?$

ADD + SUBTRACT - EQUAL = Answers: [ ]'s

1. $17.3 + 234.8 + 3.7 = ?$ **[255.8]**

2. $37.5 + 8.97 = ?$ **[46.47]**

3. $0.175 + 0.0385 = ?$ **[0.2135]**

4. $97 - 19 = ?$ **[78]**

5. $12.74 - 9.05 = ?$ **[3.69]**

6. $0.087 - 0.032 = ?$ **[0.055]**

7. $12 + 96 + 52 + 29 = ?$ **[189]**

8. $57 - 98 = ?$ **[-41]**

9. $3,979 + 4,425 = ?$ **[8,404]**

10. $28 - 12 - 17 = ?$ **[-1]**

11. $2.72 + 0.773 = ?$ **[3.493]**

12. $54,321 - 12,345 = ?$ **[41,976]**

13. $9,999 - 7,654 = ?$ **[2,345]**

Take the C2 Quiz or review.

For every positive number N there is a corresponding N negative number -N, and vice versa.

$$N + (-N) = 0 \qquad 7 + (-7) = 0$$

$$-(-N) = N \qquad -(-6) = 6$$

You may create -N from N with the $+ \leftrightarrow -$ Key located just left of the $=$ Key

$$N \underline{+ \leftrightarrow -} \text{ yields -N} \qquad 17 \underline{+ \leftrightarrow -} \text{ yields -17}$$

$$-17 \underline{+ \leftrightarrow -} \text{ yields 17}$$

Subtraction is the same as adding a negative number.

$$N - M = N + (-M) \qquad 8 - 3 = 8 + (-3) = 5$$

$$-5 - 6 = -5 + (-6) = 5 \underline{+ \leftrightarrow -} + 6 \underline{+ \leftrightarrow -} = -11$$

$$-5 \quad + \quad -6 \quad = -11$$

Play with this until you are comfortable with it. It's really easy once you catch on to it. Homework will really help here.

When you have mastered it, take the C3 Quiz.

NEGATIVE NUMBERS

1. Where is the key that creates the negative of any number in the calculator's display?

2. Create -7 in your calculator

3. $8 + (-8) = ?$

4. $9 + (-4) = ?$

5. $-(-5) = ?$

6. $-7 + (-8) = ?$

7. $18 - 11 = ?$

8. $18 + (-11) = ?$

9. $327 - 568 = ?$

10. $-13.7 + 8.5 = ?$

11. $-(-(-7)) = ?$

12. $-3 + (-4) + (-5) = ?$

NEGATIVE NUMBERS Answers: [ ]'s

1. Where is the key that creates the negative of any number in the calculator's display? [**Bottom, Left of =**]

2. Create -7 in your calculator [7 +=-]

3. 8 + (-8) = ? [0]

4. 9 + (-4) = ? [5]

5. - (-5) = ? [5]

6. -7 + (-8) = ? [-15]

7. 18 - 11 = ? [7]

8. 18 + (-11) = ? [7]

9. 327 - 568 = ? [-241]

10. -13.7 + 8.5 = ? [-5.2]

11. -(-(- 7)) = ? [-7]

12. -3 + (-4) + (-5) = ? [-12]

**Take the C3 Quiz if you are ready,
or do some more exercises, C3ES.**

NEGATIVE NUMBERS

1. $-(-(-6)) = ?$

2. Create -27 in your calculator

3. $18 + (-18) = ?$

4. $19 + (-8) = ?$

5. $- (-8) = ?$

6. $-9 + (-4) = ?$

7. $18 - 61 = ?$

8. $18 + (-61) = ?$

9. $3,827 - 968 = ?$

10. $-18.7 + 7.5 = ?$

11. $-(-(- 2.7)) = ?$

12. $-7 + (-4) + (-2) = ?$

NEGATIVE NUMBERS   Answers: [ ]'s

1. -(-(-6)) = ?   [-6]

2. Create -27 in your calculator   [27+=-]

3. 18 + (-18) = ?   [0]

4. 19 + (-8) = ?   [11]

5. - (-8) = ?   [8]

6. -9 + (-4) = ?   [-13]

7. 18 - 61 = ?   [-43]

8. 18 + (-61) = ?   [-43]

9. 3,827 - 968 = ?   [2,859]

10. -18.7 + 7.5 = ?   [-11.2]

11. -(-(- 2.7)) = ?   [-2.7]

12. -7 + (-4) + (-2) = ?   [-13]

Take the C3 Quiz or review.

We assume you know basic arithmetic operations and rules.
If not, you will need some more basic training.

Key **k** is indicated by <u>k</u> the underline.

The = Key is used to complete a calculation.

Multiplication <u>x</u> Key multiplies two numbers

$3 \underline{x} 4 = 12$ $12.5 \underline{x} 7.8 = 97.5$

$(3/8) \underline{x} (5/6) = 5/16$ (See Lesson 10 x on fractions.)

Rules:

$(-A)xB = -(AxB)$ or $(-A)B = -(AB)$
$(-A)x(-B) = AxB$ or $(-A)(-B) = AB$

Division <u>÷</u> Key Divides two numbers

A/B means A <u>÷</u> B

$12/4 = 12 ÷ 4 = 3$ $15.7 ÷ 2.8 = 5.6$

$A/(-B) = -(A/B) = (-A)/B$ $18 ÷ -6 = -3$

$(-A)/(-B) = A/B$ $(-15)/(-5) = 3$

Again, practice is the key to mastery.
Have fun with the exercises. Then take the C4 Quiz.

MULTIPLY x   DIVIDE ÷

1. 3.5 x 7.4 = ?

2. 154 x 896 = ?

3. 0.0075 x 0.02 = ?

4. -54 x 87 = ?

5. (-32) x (-76) = ?

6. 79 ÷ 3 =

7. 859 ÷ 54 = ?

8. 86 ÷ (-3) = ?

9. (-45) ÷ (-2.5) = ?

10. (87 x 34) ÷ 5 = ?

11. (5.4 x 7.1)x2.3 = ?

12. 8,754 ÷ (-23) = ?

13. (54.2 ÷ 3.4) x (8.7 ÷ (-4.3)) = ?

MULTIPLY x   DIVIDE ÷   Answers: [ ]'s

1. 3.5 x 7.4 = ?   [**25.9**]

2. 154 x 896 = ?   [**137,984**] (You put in the
                                                comma.)

3. 0.0075 x 0.02 = ?   [**0.00015**]

4. -54 x 87 = ?   [**-4,698**]

5. (-32) x (-76) = ?   [**2,432**]

6. 79 ÷ 3 =   [**26.3**]

7. 859 ÷ 54 = ?   [**15.9**]

8. 86 ÷ (-3) = ?   [**-28.7**]

9. (-45) ÷ (-2.5) = ?   [**18.0**]

10. (87 x 34) ÷ 5 = ?   [**591.6**]

11. (5.4 x 7.1)x2.3 = ?   [**88.2**]

12. 8,754 ÷ (-23) = ?   [**-381**]

13. (54.2 ÷ 3.4) x (8.7 ÷ (-4.3)) = ?   [**-32.3**]

Take the C4 Quiz or do some more exercises, C4ES.

MULTIPLY x   DIVIDE ÷

1. 3.8 x 9.4 = ?

2. 74 x 396 = ?

3. 0.0035 x 0.08 = ?

4. -59 x 27 = ?

5. (-36) x (-82) = ?

6. 89 ÷ 4 = ?

7. 869 ÷ 34 = ?

8. 88 ÷ (-3) + ?

9. (-47) ÷ (-6.5) = ?

10. [47 x 74] ÷ 6 = ?

11. (5.6 x 7.3) x 2.9 = ?

12. 8,954 ÷ (-32) = ?

13. (56.2 ÷ 3.2) x (9.7 ÷ (-2.3)) = ?

MULTIPLY x   DIVIDE ÷   Answers: [ ]'s

1. 3.8 x 9.4 = ?   [35.7]

2. 74 x 396 = ?   [29304]

3. 0.0035 x 0.08 = ?   [0.00028]

4. -59 x 27 = ?   [-1,593]

5. (-36) x (-82) = ?   [2,952]

6. 89 ÷ 4 = ?   [22.25]

7. 869 ÷ 34 = ?   [25.6]

8. 88 ÷ (-3) + ?   [-29.3]

9. (-47) ÷ (-6.5) = ?   [7.2]

10. [47 x 74] ÷ 6 = ?   [580 or 579.67]

11. (5.6 x 7.3) x 2.9 = ?   [118.6]

12. 8,954 ÷ (-32) = ?   [-280 or -279.81]

13. (56.2 ÷ 3.2) x (9.7 ÷ (-2.3)) = ?   [-74.1]

Take the C4 Quiz or review.

C5 LESSON: PERCENTAGE   %

We say X% (X Percent) of A is: (X/100)x A

30% of 100 is (30/100)x100 = .30 x 100 = 30

45% of 156 is (45/100)x156 = .45 x 156 = 70.2

There is a **%** Key on the TI-30Xa.

It is above the **2** Key. Select **2nd** then the number **2** to get it.

> 45 **2nd** **2** yields .45

So: 45 **2nd** **2** x 156 = 70.2

To add **X%** of A to A: A **+** X **2nd** **2** = (1 + X/100)A

Add 35% of 256 to itself: 256 **+** 35 **2nd** **2** = 345.6

There will be a deeper Lesson on Percentages, Discounts and Mark-ups in Tier 3 which goes into more detail on percentages.

This is just to show you how the % Key works.

PERCENTAGE %

1. Where is the % key on the TI-30Xa?

2. How do you activate the % Function?

3. What is 45% of 156?

4. Enter 45   Display is ?
   Press **2nd 2** Key   Display is ?
   Press the **x** Key   Display is ?
   Enter 156   Display is ?
   Press = Key   Display is ?

5. What is 87% of 835?

6. Add 35% of 287 to itself.

7. Enter 287   Display is ?
   Press **+** Key   Display is ?
   Enter 35   Display is ?
   Press **2nd 2** Key   Display is ?
   Press = Key   Display is ?

8. 165% of 200 is?

9. Add 80% of 125 to itself and get?

10. 4% of 1000 is?

PERCENTAGE %   Answers: [ ]'s

1. Where is the % key on the TI-30Xa? [**Above the 2**]

2. How do you activate the % Function? [**Press the yellow <u>2nd</u>**
    Then the <u>2</u> key.

3. What is 45% of 156?   [**70.2**]

4. Enter 45   Display is ?   [**45**]
    Press **2nd 2** Key   Display is ?   [**0.45**]
    Press the **x** Key   Display is ?   [**0.45**]
    Enter 156   Display is ?   [**156**]
    Press = Key   Display is ?   [**70.2**]

5. What is 87% of 835?   [**726.45**]

6. Add 35% of 287 to itself.   [**387.45**]

7. Enter 287   Display is ?   [**287**]
    Press **+** Key   Display is ?   [**287**]
    Enter 35   Display is ?   [**35**]
    Press **2nd 2** Key   Display is ?   [**100.45**]
    Press = Key   Display is ?   [**387.45**]

8. 165% of 200 is?   [**330**]

9. Add 80% of 125 to itself and get?   [**225**]

10. 4% of 1000 is?   [**40**]

Take the C5 Quiz if ready,
or do more exercises, C5ES.

PERCENTAGE %

1. What is 145% of 156?

2. Enter 145   Display is ?
   Press **2nd 2** Key   Display is ?
   Press the **x** Key   Display is ?
   Enter 156   Display is ?
   Press = Key   Display is ?

3. Enter 156   Display is ?
   Press **x** Key   Display is ?
   Enter 145   Display is ?
   Press **2nd 2** Key   Display is ?
   Press = Key   Display is ?

Do you see the two different ways?

4. What is 37**%** of 835?

5. What is 137**%** of 835

6. Add 55**%** of 287 to itself.

7. Enter 287   Display is ?
   Press **+** Key   Display is ?
   Enter 55%   Display is ?
   Press **2nd 2** Key   Display is ?
   Press = Key   Display is ?

PERCENTAGE %

Answers: [ ]'s

1. What is 145% of 156?   [226.2]

2.

Enter 145	Display is ?	[145]
Press **2nd 2** Key	Display is ?	[1.45]
Press the **x** Key	Display is ?	[1.45]
Enter 156	Display is ?	[156]
Press = Key	Display is ?	[226.2]

3.

Enter 156	Display is ?	[156]
Press **x** Key	Display is ?	[156]
Enter 145	Display is ?	[145]
Press **2nd 2** Key	Display is ?	[1.45]
Press = Key	Display is ?	[226.2]

Do you see the two different ways?

4. What is 37**%** of 835?   [308.95]

5. What is 137**%** of 835   [1,143.95 = 835 + 308.95]

6. Add 55**%** of 287 to itself.   [444.85]

7.

Enter 287	Display is ?	[287]
Press **+** Key	Display is ?	[287]
Enter 55%	Display is ?	[55]
Press **2nd 2** Key	Display is ?	[157.85]
Press = Key	Display is ?	[444.85]

Make up some problems for yourself and take the C5 Quiz.

Revised 2023-03-31

C6 LESSON: MEMORY M1, M2, M3   STO RCL (   )

Sometimes you may need to store a number in the calculator to be recalled later.

<u>STO</u> and <u>RCL</u> do this.

There are three memory registers, **M1**, **M2**, and **M3**.

To store a number <u>N</u> in memory register <u>1</u> do this:

Enter <u>N</u>, then <u>STO</u> <u>1</u> and N is stored in **M1**

Later to recall N: <u>RCL</u> <u>1</u> will restore <u>N</u>.

Example: (3 x 4) + (5 x 7) + (4 x 8)

        3 x 4 = 12 <u>STO</u> <u>1</u>,   5 x 7 = 35 <u>STO</u> <u>2</u>,   4 x 8 = 32

        Now 32 + <u>RCL</u> 1 + <u>RCL</u> 2 = 79

Or use the ( ) keys: Simply duplicate the above.

Memory is used when you need to store a number for later use. Parenthesis are used for shorter term storage in a calculation.

For example, if you need to store someone's phone number; say, 5013452314, simply enter this and <u>STO</u> <u>1</u>.

Now <u>RCL</u> <u>1</u> will recall it anytime in the future even if you turn the calculator OFF. Only storing another number in **M1** will erase it.

MEMORY M1, M2, M3 STO RCL ( )

1. How many memory registers does the TI-30Xa have?

2. Where do you see the **M1, M2,** and **M3** displayed?

3. Which keys do you use to store a number in memory **M2**?

4. Store 235 in **M2**.

5. How do you recall the number in stored in **M2**?

6. What number is in **M2**?

7. Do you lose the numbers stored in memory when you turn the calculator off?

8. How do you "clear" the memory register **M3**?

9. What can you also use for temporary memory storage when doing a calculation?

10. (12.3 + 87) x (34 + 56) = ?

Answers are in C6EA.

"Play" with the memory and ( ) until you are comfortable with them…then take the C6 Quiz.

MEMORY M1, M2, M3 STO RCL ( )   Answers: [ ]'s

1. How many memory registers does the TI-30Xa have? [**3**]

2. Where are the **M1, M2** and **M3** displayed?   [**Upper Left**]

3. Which keys do you use to store a number in
   memory **M2**?   [**STO 2**]

4. Store 235 in **M2**.   [**Enter 235 press STO 2**]

5. How do you recall the number in stored in **M2**? [**RCL 2**]

6. What number is in **M2**?   [**235**]

7. Do you lose the numbers stored in Memory when you turn the
   calculator off?   [**No**]

8. How do you "clear" the memory register M3?
                                          [**Enter 0 Press STO 3**]

9. What can you also use for temporary memory storage when
   doing a calculation?   [**( )**]

10. (12.3 + 87) x (34 + 56) = ?   [**8,937**]

**"Play" with the memory and ( ) until you are comfortable with
them…then take the C6 Quiz.**

C7 LESSON: X^2 SQUARE

Definition: A^2 = AxA...we say: **A squared**

$$5^2 = 5x5 = 25 \qquad (7.4)^2 = 7.4x7.4 = 54.8$$

An easier way to get this is the $\underline{x}^2$ key

7.4x2 yields 54.8 (or 54.76 depending on the **FIX**.)

This is handy for larger numbers.

543.7 squared is simply 543.7 $\underline{x}^2$ = 295609.69

You must supply the commas: 295,609.69

Very quick and easy and used a lot in practical math.

NOTE: $(-A)^2 = A^2$ -5 $\underline{x}^2$ = 25   So $\underline{x}^2$ result is always positive.

As usual, exercises and C7 Quiz.

x^2 SQUARE

1. What is the definition of A^2?

2. Where is the x^2 key on the TI-30Xa?

3. $(137.4)^2 = ?$

4. $(6.2)^2 = ?$

5. $(-8.7)^2 = ?$

6. $(3.4 + 8.7)^2 = ?$

7. $(5^2)^2 = ?$

8. $(78 \div 3.3)^2 = ?$

9. Can A^2 be negative?

10. $7^2 - 3^2 = ?$

11. $(((((2)^2)^2)^2)^2)^2 = ?$

$\mathbf{X^2}$ **SQUARE**   Answers: [ ]'s

1. What is the definition of A^2?   [AxA]

2. Where is the $\mathbf{x^2}$ key on the TI-30Xa? [**3 down middle**]

3. $(137.4)^2 = $?   [**18878.76 or 18,878.76**]

4. $(6.2)^2 = $?   [**38.44**]

5. $(-8.7)^2 = $?   [**75.69**]

6. $(3.4 + 8.7)^2 = $?   [**146.41**]

7. $(5^2)^2 = $?   [**625**]

8. $(78 \div 3.3)^2 = $?   [**558.7**]

9. Can A^2 be negative?   [**No**]

10. $7^2 - 3^2 = $?   [**40**]

11. $(((((2)^2)^2)^2)^2)^2 = $?   [**4,294,967,296**]

Play with x^2 Key until you have mastered it.

Take the C7 Quiz or practice some more with C7ES.

$$X^2 \quad \text{SQUARE}$$

1. $(92.56)^2 = ?$

2. $(16.2)^2 = ?$

3. $(-75.7)^2 = ?$

4. $(4.3 + 6.7)^2 = ?$

5. $(7^2)^2 = ?$

6. $(478 \div 23.3)^2 = ?$

7. Can A^2 be 0?

8. $8^2 - 12^2 = ?$

9. $(((((2.05)^2)^2)^2)^2)^2 = ?$

10. $(2 \ 3/4)^2 = ?$

X^2 **SQUARE** Answers: [ ]'s

1. $(92.56)^2 = ?$ [8,567.35]

2. $(16.2)^2 = ?$ [262.44]

3. $(-75.7)^2 = ?$ [5,730.49]

4. $(4.3 + 6.7)^2 = ?$ [121]

5. $(7^2)^2 = ?$ [2,401]

6. $(478 \div 23.3)^2 = ?$ [420.9]

7. Can A^2 be 0?   [Yes, $0^2 = 0$]

8. $8^2 - 12^2 = ?$ [-80]

9. $(((((2.05)^2)^2)^2)^2)^2 = ?$ [9,465,063,976]

    Compare to #11 on previous page!

10. $(2\ 3/4)^2 = ?$ [7 9/16 = 121/16 = 7.5625]

Play with x^2 key until you have mastered it.
Take the C7 Quiz or review.

C8 LESSON: √X SQUARE ROOT

Definition: $(\sqrt{A})^2 = A$

$\sqrt{25} = 5$ since 52 = 25

The "problem" is given A, what is $\sqrt{A}$?

In the old days, this was a difficult problem and there was not an easy way to determine it. But, today thanks to the power tool of math, the calculator, it is very easy.

Just use the √x key.

346 √x yields the answer 18.6

Also, note x^2 and $\sqrt{x}$ are "**inverses**."

This was revolutionary in the 1970's. It changed many ways we taught engineering and science subjects along with the trig functions.

NOTE: You may not take the square root of a negative number with this calculator. The square root of a negative number exists, but it is not a real number. It is called a complex or imaginary number and will require a more sophisticated power tool. See Tier 4.

For now, -7 √x yields an "Error" message.

As usual, Exercises and the C8 Quiz.

√**X**   SQUARE ROOT

1. Define $\sqrt{A}$

2. $\sqrt{36} = ?$

3. $\sqrt{137} = ?$

4. $\sqrt{19.4} = ?$

5. $\sqrt{(5.4 + 87.2)} = ?$

6. $(\sqrt{76})^2 = ?$

7. $\sqrt{(35)^2} = ?$

8. $\sqrt{-73} = ?$

9. $\sqrt{(\sqrt{98})} = ?$

10. $\sqrt{98765432} = ?$

√**X** SQUARE ROOT   Answers: [ ]'s

1. Define $\sqrt{A}$ $[(\sqrt{A})^2 = A]$

2. $\sqrt{36} = ?$ $[6]$

3. $\sqrt{137} = ?$ $[11.7]$

4. $\sqrt{19.4} = ?$ $[4.4]$

5. $\sqrt{(5.4 + 87.2)} = ?$ $[9.6]$

6. $(\sqrt{76})^2 = ?$ $[76]$

7. $\sqrt{(35)^2} = ?$ $[35]$

8. $\sqrt{-73} = ?$ [**Error**] Why?

9. $\sqrt{(\sqrt{98})} = ?$ $[3.15]$

10. $\sqrt{98765432} = ?$ $[9,938]$

Play with √ until you are comfortable with it.

Take the C8 Quiz or do some more exercises, C8ES.

√X   SQUARE ROOT

1. Define $\sqrt{A}$

2. $\sqrt{256} = ?$

3. $\sqrt{1,000,000} = ?$

4. $\sqrt{1,000} = ?$

5. $\sqrt{1,024} = ?$

6. $(\sqrt{1,776})^2 = ?$

7. $\sqrt{(\sqrt{(\sqrt{(\sqrt{(\sqrt{4,294,967,296})})})})} = ?$

8. $\sqrt{-(-81)} = ?$

9. $\sqrt{(\sqrt{81})} = ?$

10. $\sqrt{987,654,321} = ?$

C8ESA

√**X**   **SQUARE ROOT**   Answers: [ ]'s

1. Define √A $[\sqrt{A} \times \sqrt{A} = A]$

2. √256 = ?   [16]

3. √1,000,000 = ?   [1,000]

4. √1,000 = ?   [31.6]

5. √1,024 = ?   [32]

6. $(\sqrt{1{,}776})^2$ = ?   [1,776]

7. √(√(√(√(√4,294,967,296)))) = ?   [2]

8. √-(-81) = ?   [9]

9. √(√81) = ?   [3]

10. √987,654,321 = ? $[31{,}427 \sim 10{,}000\pi]$

Play with √ until you are comfortable with it.

Take the C8 Quiz or review.

C9 LESSON: 1/X   RECIPROCAL   "FLIP IT"

$1 \div x$ is called the "reciprocal." Thus, $1/5 = .2$.

Now the **1/x** Key makes calculating it easy.

> 5 **1/x** yields .2

> 7 **1/x** yields .142857143 or .143 or .14 (**FIX**)

> **NOTE:** 1/x is its own inverse;   N **1/x 1/x** yields N…You try it!

To recap our progress so far:

> $+$ $-$ x $\div$ x^2 $\sqrt{x}$ $1/x$ $=$ are the eight
"**work horse**" keys of practical math.

Learn them well. They are your friends.

The ( ) and **RCL** and **STO** will help sometimes.

So far, we have dealt only with real numbers expressed as base ten decimal numbers. This is often all you will ever need. But; sometimes, we express numbers as fractions. There are some wonderful keys that will help here too. (**See C10, C11, and C12**)

1/X   RECIPROCAL   "FLIP IT"

1. Define 1/x

2. 1/89 = ?

3. 1 ÷ 89 = ?

4. The reciprocal of 3 is ?

5. 1/1/79 = ?

6. 1/1/S = ?

7. 1/0.7 = ?

8. 1/0.07 = ?

9. 1/0.007 = ?

10. $1/(3^2 + 4^2)$ = ?

11. $\sqrt{[1/25]}$ = ?

12. $(1/25)^2$ = ?

1/X   RECIPROCAL   "FLIP IT"   Answers: [ ]'s

1. Define 1/x $[1 \div x]$

2. 1/89 = ? $[0.011]$

3. $1 \div 89$ = ? $[0.011]$

4. The reciprocal of 3 is ? $[1/3 = 0.33]$

5. 1/1/79 = ? $[79]$

6. 1/1/S = ? $[S]$

7. 1/0.7 = ? $[1.429]$

8. 1/0.07 = ? $[14.29]$

9. 1/0.007 = ? $[142.9]$

10. $1/(3^2 + 4^2)$ = ? $[0.04 \text{ or } 1/25]$

11. $\sqrt{[1/25]}$ = ? $[0.2]$

12. $(1/25)^2$ = ? $[0.0016]$

Play with 1/x

Take the C9 Quiz or do more exercises, C9ES.

1/X   RECIPROCAL   "FLIP IT"

1. $1/0 = ?$

2. $1/1 = ?$

3. $1/0.5 = ?$

4. $1/(1/2) = ?$

5. $1/1/9 = ?$

6. $1/1/A = ?$

7. $1/(3 + 4) = ?$

8. $1/\sqrt{16} = ?$

9. $1/(1 + 2 + 3) = ?$

10. $1/1/1/1/1/3 = ?$

11. $1/1/1/1/1/1/3 = ?$

12. $(1/7)^2 = ?$

1/X   RECIPROCAL "FLIP IT"   Answers: [ ]'s

1. $1/0$ = ?   [Error]

2. $1/1$ = ?   [1]

3. $1/0.5$ = ?   [2]

4. $1/(1/2)$ = ?   [2]

5. $1/1/9$ = ?   [9]

6. $1/1/A$ = ?   [A]

7. $1/(3 + 4)$ = ?   [0.14]

8. $1/\sqrt{16}$ = ?   [0.25]

9. $1/(1 + 2 + 3)$ = ?   [1/6 = 0.166667]

10. $1/1/1/1/1/3$ = ?   [0.3333]

11. $1/1/1/1/1/1/3$ = ?   [3]

12. $(1/7)^2$ = ?   [0.02]

Play with 1/x
Take the C9 Quiz or review.

Let's quickly review fractions. Let A and B be two **integers**.
Then, A/B is called a **fraction**. If A > B then this fraction is
greater than 1 and called **improper**. There are four rules for
adding, subtracting, multiplying and dividing fractions you should
know.

$$A/B + C/D = (AD + BC)/BD$$
$$A/B - C/D = (AD - BC)/BD$$
$$A/BxC/D = AC/BD$$
$$(A/B)/(C/D) = A/BxD/C$$

$$2/3 + 4/5 = (2x5 + 3x4)/3x5 = (10+12)/15 =$$
$$22/15 = 1\ 7/15$$

The $\underline{a}^{b/c}$ lets you enter the two fractions and add them. Watch
the video to see how.

Similarly you can subtract, multiply, and divide two fractions.
See the video. **Do the exercises**.

The largest denominator you may enter is 999. So, if you should
multiply two fractions resulting in a denominator greater than
999, the answer will be in decimal form.

Also, you may apply the other function keys to fractions just like
any other number.

FRACTIONS $a^{b/c}$ + - X ÷ 1/X

1. 3/4 + 7/8 = ?

2. 7/8 - 2/3 = ?

3. 2/3x4/5 = ?

4. 5/6 ÷ 2/3 = ?

5. -5/6 x 2/3 = ?

6. -3/4 x -2/3 = ?

7. 1/(2/3) = ?

8. $(6/7)^2$ = ?

9. √(5/6) = ?

10. What is largest denominator you can enter for a fraction with the TI-30Xa?

11. 17/8 + 13/3 = ?

12. 5/6 ÷ 7/9 = ?

FRACTIONS $a^{b/c}$ **+ - X ÷ 1/X**   Answers: [ ]'s

1. 3/4 + 7/8 = ?   [1 5/8 = 13/8 = 1.625]

2. 7/8 - 2/3 = ?   [5/24]

3. 2/3x4/5 = ?   [8/15]

4. 5/6 ÷ 2/3 = ?   [1 1/4 = 5/4 = 1.25]

5. -5/6 x 2/3 = ?   [-5/9]

6. -3/4 x -2/3 = ?   [1/2]

7. 1/(2/3) = ?   [1.5 = 1 1/2 = 3/2]

8. $(6/7)^2$ = ?   [0.734693878 = 36/49]

9. √(5/6) = ?   [0.91287]

10. What is largest denominator you can enter for a fraction with the TI-30Xa?   [999]

11. 17/8 + 13/3 = ?   [6 11/24 = 155/24 = 6.46]

12. 5/6 ÷ 7/9 = ?   [1 1/14 = 15/14 = 1.07]

Play with fractions.

Take the C10 Quiz or do more exercises, C10ES.

FRACTIONS $a^{b/c}$ + - X ÷ 1/X

1. 3/7 + 7/8 = ?

2. 7/8 - 5/6 = ?

3. 2/3 x 2/5 = ?

4. 5/9 ÷ 2/3 = ?

5. -5/6 x 4/3 = ?

6. -5/4 x -2/3 = ?

7. 1/(2/7) = ?

8. $(5/7)^2$ = ?

9. $\sqrt{(4/7)}$ = ?

10. What is largest denominator you can enter for a fraction with the TI-30Xa?

11. 1 7/8 + 2 3/4 = ?

12. 5/8 ÷ 7/12 = ?

FRACTIONS $a^{b/c}$ + - X ÷ 1/X   Answers: [ ]'s

1. 3/7 + 7/8 = ?   [1 17/56 = 73/56 = 1.30]

2. 7/8 - 5/6 = ?   [1/24]

3. 2/3 x 2/5 = ?   [4/15]

4. 5/9 ÷ 2/3 = ?   [5/6]

5. -5/6 x 4/3 = ?   [-1 1/9 = -10/9 = -1.11]

6. -5/4 x -2/3 = ?   [5/6]

7. 1/(2/7) = ?   [3.5 = 3 1/2 = 7/2]

8. $(5/7)^2$ = ?   [25/49 = 0.51]

9. √(4/7) = ?   [0.756]

10. What is largest denominator you can enter for a fraction with the TI-30Xa?   [999]

11. 1 7/8 + 2 3/4 = ?   [4 5/8= 4.625]

12. 5/8 ÷ 7/12 = ?   [1.07 = 15/14 = 1 1/14]

Play with fractions.
Take the C10 Quiz or review.

C11 LESSON: D/C   PROPER / IMPROPER FRACTION

"d/c" is a yellow "key" seen above the $a^{b/c}$ key. You get to it by selecting 2nd $a^{b/c}$.

If A < B,   A/B is called a proper fraction.   (6/8)

If A > B,   A/B is called an improper fraction. (8/6)

A Mixed Fraction is an integer plus a fraction like 2 3/4.

If A and B share no common factor we say A/B is reduced to lowest terms.   6/8 = 3/4 in lowest terms.

The d/c Key does this plus more. It is **2nd** $a^{b/c}$.

Enter 2 3/6 as a mixed fraction (watch video) .

Hit the d/c Key and get 15/6...**again**...2 1/2...**again**...5/2.

So you first get an improper, then mixed lowest terms and then improper lowest.

Play with it. Do some exercises. Have fun.

Remember...largest denominator is 999, otherwise it will convert automatically to decimal. (See next Lesson, C12.)

D/C PROPER/IMPROPER FRACTION

1. Where is the "d/c" Key or Function?
   Express the answer as an improper fraction and a mixed fraction.

2. 3/4 + 4/5 = ?

3. 2/3 ÷ 4/7 = ?

4. 1 2/3 + 3 3/4 = ?

5. 6 7/8 − 2 2/3 = ?

6. $(2 \ 3/4)^2$ = ?

7. -(6/7) x 13/8

8. 2 x 4 3/4 = ?

9. 15/7 + 2 3/4 + 12/5 = ?

10. 2 3/4 ÷ 15/7 = ?

11. √(7/4 - 5/13) = ?

12. $\sqrt{(3^2 + 4^2)}$ = ?

D/C PROPER/IMPROPER FRACTION   Answers: [ ]'s

1. Where is the "d/c" Key or Function?   [2nd ab/c]
   Express the answer as an improper fraction and a mixed fraction.

2. 3/4 + 4/5 = ?   [31/20 = 1 11/20]

3. 2/3 ÷ 4/7 = ?   [7/6 = 1 1/6]

4. 1 2/3 + 3 3/4 = ?   [65/12 = 5 5/12]

5. 6 7/8 − 2 2/3 = ?   [101/24 = 4 5/24]

6. (2 3/4)^2 = ?   [121/16 = 7 9/16 = 7.5625]

7. -(6/7) x 13/8   [-39/28 = -1 11/28]

8. 2 x 4 3/4 = ?   [19/2 = 9 1/2]

9. 15/7 + 2 3/4 + 12/5 = ?   [1021/140 = 7 41/140]

10. 2 3/4 ÷ 15/7 = ?   [77/60 = 1 17/60]

11. √(7/4 - 5/13) = ?   [1.17]

12. √(3^2 + 4^2) = ?   [5]

NOTE: In Question 6, the answer is 7.5625. In Lesson 12, you will learn how to convert 79/16 to a decimal.

Take the C11 Quiz or do more exercises, C11ES

D/C PROPER/IMPROPER FRACTION

1. Where is the "F <--> D" Key or Function?

    In the following questions, express the answer as an improper fraction and a mixed fraction.

2. $3/7 + 17/21 = ?$

3. $2/3 \div 2/7 = ?$

4. $2 \; 2/3 + 5 \; 3/4 = ?$

5. $4 \; 7/8 - 2 \; 2/5 = ?$

6. $(2 \; 3/5)^2 = ?$

7. $-(6/7) \times 1 \; 3/8$

8. $3.5 \times 3 \; 3/5 = ?$

9. $1 \; 5/7 + 2 \; 3/4 + 12/5 = ?$

10. $3 \; 3/4 \div 13/7 = ?$

11. $\sqrt{(17/5 - 2/13)} = ?$

12. $\sqrt{\{(1/3)^2 + (1/4)^2)\}} = ?$

D/C PROPER/IMPROPER FRACTION   Answers: [ ]'s

1. Where is the "F <--> D" Key or Function?

                         [2nd <-----]   [Lower Left Corner]

   In the following questions, express the answer as an improper fraction and a mixed fraction.

2. $3/7 + 17/21 = ?$ [1 5/21 = 26/21]

3. $2/3 \div 2/7 = ?$ [2 1/3 = 7/3]

4. $2\ 2/3 + 5\ 3/4 = ?$ [8 5/12 = 101/12]

5. $4\ 7/8 - 2\ 2/5 = ?$ [2 19/40 = 99/40]

6. $(2\ 3/5)^2 = ?$ [6 19/25 = 169/25 = 6.76]

7. $-(6/7)\ \text{x}\ 1\ 3/8$ [-1 5/28 = -33/28]

8. $3.5\ \text{x}\ 3\ 3/5 = ?$ [12 3/5 = 63/5]

9. $1\ 5/7 + 2\ 3/4 + 12/5 = ?$ [6 121/140 = 961/140]

10. $3\ 3/4 \div 13/7 = ?$ [2 1/52 = 105/52]

11. $\sqrt{(17/5 - 2/13)} = ?$ [1.8]

12. $\sqrt{\{(1/3)^2 + (1/4)^2)\}} = ?$ [0.417 = 5/12]

NOTE: In Question 6, the answer is 6.76. In Lesson 12, you will learn how to convert 169/25 to a decimal.

Take the C11 Quiz or review.

Revised 2023-03-31

C12 LESSON: F ↔ D   FRACTION TO DECIMAL CONVERSION

Any fraction can be converted to a decimal, although sometimes it will only be an approximation.

$$1/2 = .5 \text{ exactly}, \quad 1/3 = .3333 \text{ approximately.}$$

This can be accomplished automatically with the **F ↔ D** yellow "Key" via **2nd** ← .

2/3 **F ↔ D** .66667 depending on the **FIX**.

F ↔ D again and you get 2/3 back.

Warning. If you enter .66667 and then **F ↔ D**, nothing will happen…no fraction. **F ↔ D** only works when you **start** with a fraction.

So, it is convenient when you want to end up with a decimal.

Ex: 8/15 + 9/17 = 116/255… you want the decimal equivalent.

Just **F ↔ D** and get 1.06275 (depending on **FIX**)

Also, you can go back, and then use **d/c** to get 271/255.

Again, **have fun** with some exercises and it will soon be very easy to use these three keys. Even if you can "do" fractions manually, this will be much faster and more error free. That's the point of a "power tool."

F ↔ D FRACTION TO DECIMAL CONVERSION

1. Where is the F ↔ D "Key" or Function?

2. Convert 3/7 to decimal

3. Convert 0.375 to fraction

4. Convert 1/3 to decimal

5. Convert 0.33 to fraction

6. Convert 0.333 to fraction

7. What Happened? Why not 1/3?

8. What is largest denominator you can enter?

9. Can you get 3/250 + 4/7 in fraction form?

10. Convert 568/126 to improper fraction in lowest terms.

F ↔ D   FRACTION TO DECIMAL CONVERSION

Answers: [ ]'s

1. Where is the F ↔ D "Key" or Function?

     [2nd ← Bottom Left of Keypad]

2. Convert 3/7 to decimal   [0.4286]

3. Convert 0.375 to fraction   [3/8]

4. Convert 1/3 to decimal   [0.33333333]

5. Convert 0.33 to fraction   [33/100]

6. Convert 0.333 to fraction   [0.333]

7. What Happened? Why not 1/3?

     [Denominator would be 1000, larger than 999]

8. What is largest denominator you can enter?   [999]

9. Can you get 3/250 + 4/7 in fraction form?

     [No, not with the TI-30Xa.
     (3x7 + 4x250)/1750 = 1021/1750 = 0.5834]

10. Convert 568/126 to improper fraction in lowest terms.
                    [284/63]

Take C12 Quiz or do some more exercises, C12ES.

F ↔ D   FRACTION TO DECIMAL CONVERSION

1. Convert 7/3 to decimal

2. Convert 3/8 to decimal

3. Convert 0.385 to fraction

4. Convert 2 1/3 to decimal

5. Convert 3 1/7 to decimal

6. Convert 0.044 to fraction

7. Convert 0.0444 to fraction

8. What Happened?

9. What is largest denominator for the TI-30Xa?

10. Can you get 3/250 + 4/7 in fraction form?

11. Convert 476/252 to improper fraction in lowest terms.

F ↔ D   FRACTION TO DECIMAL CONVERSION

Answers: [ ]'s

1. Convert 7/3 to decimal   [2.33]

2. Convert 3/8 to decimal   [0.375]

3. Convert 0.385 to fraction   [77/200]

4. Convert 2 1/3 to decimal   [2.333]

5. Convert 3 1/7 to decimal   [3.1428]

6. Convert 0.044 to fraction   [11/250]

7. Convert 0.0444 to fraction   [0.0444]

8. What Happened?   [Too large a denominator]

9. What is largest denominator for the TI-30Xa?   [999]

10. Can you get 3/250 + 4/7 in fraction form?   [No]

11. Convert 476/252 to improper fraction in lowest terms.
                    [17/9]

Take the C12 Quiz or review.

C13 LESSON: DEG   RAD   GRAD   THREE ANGLE MEASURES

There are three measures of an angle acceptable by the TI-30Xa calculator.

Degree   **DEG**   1/360 of a circle

Gradian   **GRAD**   1/400 of a circle

Radian   **RAD** $1/2\pi$ of a circle with radius 1. (57.3 DEG)

In our Practical Math Foundation we will only use the **DEG** which is what automatically comes up when you turn on the calculator.

The **DRG** Key changes the choice of unit.

If you enter a number in the **DEG** mode and then press the **2nd DRG** Keys, you will transform the number to the new unit.

For example, enter 180 as **DEG**, then transform into **RAD** (3.1416) and **GRAD** (200)

Or; enter 1 in **RAD** mode, and transform into 57.3 Degrees.

We will only use **DEG** in the Foundation training.

RAD will also be used in Tiers 4 and up. It is the "natural" measurement of an angle for trig and calculus.

DEG RAD GRAD THREE ANGLE MEASURES

1. DEG stands for?

2. What fraction of a circle is one degree?

3. What are the other two angle measures on the TI-30Xa calculator?

4. Which measure comes up when you turn on the calculator?

5. How do you switch to the other two measures?

6. How do you convert Degrees to **RAD**s and **GRAD**s?

7. How many **RAD**s are 90 degrees?

8. How many **GRAD**s are 90 degrees?

9. What will we use exclusively in the Foundations Course to measure angles?

Answers are in C13EA.

Take the C13 Quiz.

DEG RAD GRAD THREE ANGLE MEASURES

Answers: [ ]'s

1. DEG stands for?   [**Degree** °]

2. What fraction of a circle is one degree? [**1/360**]

3. What are the other two angle measures on the
    TI-30Xa calculator?   [**RAD and GRAD**]

4. Which measure comes up when you turn on the calculator?
                                                        [**DEG**]

5. How do you switch to the other two measures?
                          [**Press the DRG key once for RAD again
                          for GRAD and again for DEG**]

6. How do you convert Degrees to RADs and GRADs?
                          [**Enter the degrees and press the 2nd
                          DEG key for RADs and press 2nd DEG
                          key again for GRADs**]

7. How many RADs are 90 degrees?   [**1.57**]

8. How many GRADs are 90 degrees?   [**100**]

9. What will we use exclusively in the Foundations Course to
    measure angles?   [**DEG Degrees**]

Take the C13 Quiz or review.

C14 LESSON: SIN   SIN^{-1}

These two keys are used to compute the Sine of an angle, and the angle, if you know its <u>SIN</u>.

This is used in Trigonometry, and also for some interesting formulas in Geometry.

We will always use the Degree, **DEG**, measure of an angle in the Foundation course.

Enter the angle, say, θ, and press <u>SIN</u>

Example: 45 <u>SIN</u> yields .707

<u>SIN</u> (θ) is always between -1 and 1.

<u>SIN</u>$^{-1}$ is the "inverse" of the <u>SIN</u>,   <u>2nd</u> <u>SIN</u>

If <u>SIN</u> (θ) = N, then   <u>SIN</u>$^{-1}$(N) = θ

Example: <u>SIN</u>$^{-1}$(.707) = 45°

<u>SIN</u>$^{-1}$(N) only works for N between -1 and 1.

NOTE: <u>SIN</u> 135 = 0.707...in general, <u>SIN</u> (180°- θ) = <u>SIN</u> (θ)

SIN   SIN^{-1}

1. **SIN** (45°) = ?

2. **SIN** (0°) = ?

3. **Sin** (10°) = ?

4. **SIN** (30°) = ?

5. **SIN** (60°) = ?

6. **SIN** (75°) = ?

7. **SIN** (85°) = ?

8. **SIN** (90°) = ?

9. **SIN** (95°) = ?

11. **SIN** (120°) = ?

12. **SIN**$^{-1}(0.5)$ = ?

13. What angle X, has **SIN** (X) = 0.4 ?

14. **SIN**$^{-1}(0.4)$ = ?

15. **SIN**$^{-1}[$**SIN**$(50^\circ)]$ = ?

SIN   SIN⁻¹   Answers: [ ]'s

1. SIN (45°) = ?   [0.707]

2. SIN (0°) = ?   [0]

3. Sin (10°) = ?   [0.174]

4. SIN (30°) = ?   [0.500]

5. SIN (60°) = ?   [0.866]

6. SIN (75°) = ?   [0.966]

7. SIN (85°) = ?   [0.996]

8. SIN (90°) = ?   [1]

9. SIN (95°) = ?   [0.996]

11. SIN (120°) = ?   [0.866]

12. SIN⁻¹(0.5) = ?   [30 degrees]

13. What angle X, has SIN (X) = 0.4 ?   [23.58 degrees]

14. SIN⁻¹(0.4) = ?   [23.58 degrees]

15. SIN⁻¹[SIN(50°)] = ?   [50 degrees]

Take C14 Quiz or do more exercises, C14ES.

SIN   SIN⁻¹

1. $SIN(30° + 90°) = ?$

2. $SIN(45° + 90°) = ?$

3. $SIN(60° + 90°) = ?$

4. $SIN(90° + 90°) = ?$

5. $SIN^{-1}(0.866) = ?$

6. Why the discrepancy in #5?

7. $SIN^{-1}(0.5) = ?$

8. What angle X, has $SIN(X) = 0.3$?

9. $SIN^{-1}(0.3) = ?$

10. $SIN^{-1}[SIN(x°)] = ?$

11. $SIN[SIN^{-1}(x) = ?$

12. $SIN(\theta)$ is always between?

13. $SIN^{-1}(1.5) = ?$

SIN   SIN⁻¹   Answers: [ ]'s

1. SIN $(30° + 90°)$ = ?   [SIN$(120°)$ = 0.866]

2. SIN $(45° + 90°)$ = ?   [SIN$(135°)$ = 0.707]

3. SIN $(60° + 90°)$ = ?   [SIN$(150°)$ = 0.5]

4. SIN $(90° + 90°)$ = ?   [SIN$(180°)$ = 0]

5. SIN⁻¹ (0.866) = ?   [59.99° ~ 60°]

6. Why the discrepancy in #5? [**Round off error**
                      SIN$(60°)$ = 0.866025404
                      SIN$(59.99°)$ = 0.865938124]

7. SIN⁻¹(0.5) = ?   [30°]

8. What angle X, has **SIN**(X) = 0.3?   [17.5°]

9. SIN⁻¹(0.3) = ?   [17.5°]

10. SIN⁻¹[SIN$(x°)$] = ?   [x°]

11. SIN[SIN⁻¹(x) = ?   [x]

12. **SIN** $(θ)$ is always between?   [-1 and 1]

13. SIN⁻¹(1.5) = ?   [**Error**]

Take C14 Quiz or review.

Revised 2023-03-31

C15 LESSON: COS   COS^{-1}

These two keys are used to compute the Cosine of an angle, and the angle, if you know its <u>COS</u>.

This is used in Trigonometry and also for some interesting formulas in Geometry.

We will always use the Degree, **DEG**, measure of an angle in the Foundation course.

Enter the angle, say, θ, and Press <u>COS</u>

Example: 45 <u>COS</u> yields .707

<u>COS</u> (θ) is always between -1 and 1.

<u>COS</u>$^{-1}$ is the "inverse" of the <u>COS</u>, <u>2nd</u> <u>COS</u>

If <u>COS</u> (θ) = N, then **COS**$^{-1}$(N) = θ   N between -1 and 1

Example: <u>COS</u>-1(.707) = 45°

NOTE: <u>COS</u> 135 = -.707   In general, <u>COS</u> (180° - θ) = - <u>COS</u>(θ)

You could verify: <u>COS</u>(90 - θ) = **SIN** (θ) for example.

SIN and <u>COS</u> are intimately related as you will learn in the Trigonometry section of Tier 2, and even more in Tier 4.

COS   COS⁻¹

1. $\cos(45^\circ)$ = ?

2. $\cos(0^\circ)$ = ?

3. $\cos(10^\circ)$ = ?

4. $\cos(30^\circ)$ = ?

5. $\cos(60^\circ)$ = ?

6. $\cos(75^\circ)$ = ?

7. $\cos(85^\circ)$ = ?

8. $\cos(90^\circ)$ = ?

9. $\cos(95^\circ)$ = ?

10. $\cos^{-1}(0.5)$ = ?

11. What angle X, has $\cos(X) = 0.4$?

14. $\cos^{-1}(0.4)$ = ?

15. $\cos^{-1}[\sin(50^\circ)]$ = ?

COS COS⁻¹   Answers: [ ]'s

1. **COS** $(45^\circ) = ?$ [0.707]

2. **COS** $(0^\circ) = ?$ [1]

3. **COS** $(10^\circ) = ?$ [0.985]

4. **COS** $(30^\circ) = ?$ [0.866]

5. **COS** $(60^\circ) = ?$ [0.500]

6. **COS** $(75^\circ) = ?$ [0.259]

7. **COS** $(85^\circ) = ?$ [0.087]

8. **COS** $(90^\circ) = ?$ [0]

9. **COS** $(95^\circ) = ?$ [-0.087]

10. **COS⁻¹** $(0.5) = ?$ [60 degrees]

11. What angle X, has **COS** $(X) = 0.4?$ [66.4 degrees]

14. **COS⁻¹** $(0.4) = ?$ [66.4 degrees]

15. **COS⁻¹** $[SIN(50^\circ)] = ?$ [40 degrees]

Take the C15 Quiz or do some more exercise, C15ES.

COS   COS^{-1}

1. COS $(30° + 90°) = ?$

2. COS $(45° + 90°) = ?$

3. COS $(60° + 90°) = ?$

4. COS $(90° + 90°) = ?$

5. COS^{-1} $(0.866) = ?$

6. COS$^{-1}(0) = ?$

7. COS$^{-1}(0.5) = ?$

8. What angle X, has COS $(X) = 0.3?$

9. COS$^{-1}(0.3) = ?$

10. COS^{-1} [COS$(x°)$] = ?

11. COS[COS$^{-1}(x) = ?$

12. COS (θ) is always between?

13. COS$^{-1}(1.5) = ?$

COS   COS⁻¹   Answers: [ ]'s

1. COS $(30° + 90°)$ = ?   [COS($120°$) = -0.5]

2. COS $(45° + 90°)$ = ?   [COS($135°$) = -0.707]

3. COS $(60° + 90°)$ = ?   [COS($150°$) = -0.866]

4. COS $(90° + 90°)$ = ?   [COS($180°$) = -1]

5. COS⁻¹ (0.866) = ?   [$30°$]

6. COS⁻¹(0) = ?   [$90°$]

7. COS⁻¹(0.5) = ?   [$60°$]

8. What angle X, has COS (X) = 0.3?   [$72.5°$]

9. COS⁻¹(0.3) = ?   [$72.5°$]

10. COS⁻¹ [COS$(x°)$] = ?   [$x°$]

11. COS[COS⁻¹(x) = ?   [x]

12. COS $(θ)$ is always between?   [-1 and 1]

13. COS⁻¹(1.5) = ?   [Error]

Take the C15 Quiz or review.

Revised 2023-03-31

C16 LESSON: TAN   TAN^{-1}

These two keys are used to compute the Tangent of an angle, and the angle, if you know its **TAN**

This is used in Trigonometry.

We will always use the Degree, **DEG**, measure of an angle in the Foundation course.

Enter the angle, say, θ, and Press **TAN**

        Example: 45 **TAN** yields 1

TAN (θ) can be any size

TAN^{-1} is the "**inverse**" of the **TAN**, **2nd TAN**

If **TAN** (θ) = N, then **TAN^{-1}**(N) = θ

        Example: **TAN^{-1}**(1) = 45°

NOTE: We will not use **TAN** in the Foundation Course.

TAN is also intimately related to **SIN** and **COS**.

TAN   TAN^{-1}

1. TAN (45°) = ?

2. TAN (0°) = ?

3. TAN (10°) = ?

4. TAN (30°) = ?

5. TAN (60°) = ?

6. TAN (75°) = ?

7. TAN (85°) = ?

8. TAN (90°) = ?

9. TAN (95°) = ?

10. TAN^{-1} (0.5) = ?

11. What angle X, has TAN (X) = 0.4?

12. TAN^{-1}(0.4) = ?

13. TAN^{-1}[TAN(50°)] = ?

TAN   TAN⁻¹   Answers: [ ]'s

1. TAN (45°) = ?   [1]

2. TAN (0°) = ?   [0]

3. TAN (10°) = ?   [0.176]

4. TAN (30°) = ?   [0.577]

5. TAN (60°) = ?   [1.732]

6. TAN (75°) = ?   [3.732]

7. TAN (85°) = ?   [11.430]

8. TAN (90°) = ?   [Error]

9. TAN (95°) = ?   [-11.430]

10. TAN⁻¹ (0.5) = ?   [26.57°]

11. What angle X, has **TAN** (X) = 0.4?   [21.8°]

12. TAN⁻¹(0.4) = ?   [21.8°]

13. TAN⁻¹[TAN(50°)] = ?   [50°]

Take the C16 Quiz or do more exercise, C16ES.

TAN   TAN^{-1}

1. **TAN** (90°) = ?

2. **TAN** (89.99°) = ?

3. **TAN** (-89.99°) = ?

4. **TAN** (88°) = ?

5. **TAN** (80°) = ?

6. **TAN** (60°) = ?

7. **TAN** (30°) = ?

8. **TAN** (10°) = ?

9. **TAN**$^{-1}$ (0.577) = ?

10. What angle X, has **TAN** (X) = 1 ?

11. **TAN**$^{-1}$$(1)$ = ?

12. **TAN**$^{-1}$[**TAN**(150°)] = ?

13. **TAN**$^{-1}$[**TAN**(-30°)] = ?

TAN   **TAN**$^{-1}$ Answers: [ ]'s

1. TAN $(90°)$ = ?   [Error]

2. TAN $(89.99°)$ = ?   [5,729.6]

3. TAN $(-89.99°)$ = ?   [-5,729.6]

4. TAN $(88°)$ = ?   [28.6]

5. TAN $(80°)$ = ?   [5.7]

6. TAN $(60°)$ = ?   [1.7]

7. TAN $(30°)$ = ?   [0.577]

8. TAN $(10°)$ = ?   [0.176]

9. TAN^{-1} (0.577) = ?   [30°]

10. What angle X, has **TAN** (X) = 1 ?   [45°]

11. TAN$^{-1}(1)$ = ?   [45°]

12. TAN^{-1}[TAN$(150°)$] = ?   [-30°]

13. TAN^{-1}[TAN$(-30°)$] = ?   [-30°]

Take the C16 Quiz or review.

PRE-ALGEBRA INTRODUCTION

In this Foundation course we will be dealing with what are commonly called "Real Numbers" which consist of:

Integers or Whole Numbers, both positive and negative.

Fractions, or quotients, or ratios of integers.

We will usually express numbers in the standard decimal format such as:

$$327.45 = 3 \times 100 + 2 \times 10 + 7 + .4 + .05 \text{ where}$$
$$.4 = 3/10 \text{ and } .5 = 5/100$$

The Real Numbers correspond to points on a straight line.

There are four basic arithmetic operations: $+ - x \div$ and a few higher level operations such as: x^2 $1/x$ $\sqrt{x}$

There are several "Rules" or "Laws" of arithmetic.

We assume you already know most of this and will review it briefly in the following Pre-algebra lessons. See the Table of Contents for a listing of the lessons.

We will use the TI-30Xa calculator for most of the calculations we perform in this Foundations Course since it accelerates the learning and application of what you will be learning significantly.

The Keys to perform these operations have been discussed in the Lessons on the use of the TI-30Xa calculator.

Exercises Introduction

Why do the Exercises?

Mathematics is like a "game." The more you practice and play the game the better you will understand and play it.

The Foundation's Exercises, which accompany each lesson, are designed to reinforce the ideas presented to you in that lesson's video.

It is unlikely you will learn math very well by simply reading about it or listening to Dr. Del, or anyone else, or watching someone else doing it.

You WILL learn math by "doing math."

It is like learning to play a musical instrument, or write a book, or play a sport, or play chess, or cooking.

You will learn by practice.

Repetition is the key to mastery.

You will make mistakes. You will sometimes struggle to master a concept or technique. You may feel frustration sometimes "WE ALL DO."

But, as you learn and do math, you will begin to find pleasure and enjoyment in it as you would in any worthwhile endeavor. Treat it like a sport or game.

These Exercises are the KEY to your SUCCESS!

ENJOY

P1 LESSON: REAL NUMBERS, INTEGERS AND RATIONALS

First, there are the "counting numbers," 1, 2, 3, 4...also called Natural Numbers and Positive Integers.

We count with the usual decimal system which you should know.

Then we have the number Zero (0) which signifies the absence of something.

Then there are the "negative integers." These are just like the integers; but, have a $-$ sign in front of them, e.g., -5, -6 . . .

Then there are the "fractions" or "rational" numbers which are the ratios or quotients of integers, 3/4, -7/8, 15/7, etc.

We will usually express numbers in the standard decimal format such as:

$$327.45 = 3 \times 100 + 2 \times 10 + 7 + .4 + .05 \text{ where}$$

$$.4 = 4/10 \text{ and } .05 = 5/100$$

It is sometimes easiest to understand these numbers when they are corresponded to points on a straight line, see the next lesson P2.

Later we will review the various operations and "rules" of arithmetic.

Always use the calculator to help yourself understand the various things we are discussing.

We assume this is essentially a review for things you already have learned.

ARITHMETIC REVIEW

1. What kind of numbers will we deal with in the Foundation Course?

2. What are Integers?

3. What are Rational Numbers?

4. What number is 3x100 + 2x10 + 7 + 0.4 + 0.05?

5. What do the Real Numbers correspond to?

6. What are the four basic operations?

7. What calculator will we use in the Foundation Course?

8. What other three subjects will we learn about in the Foundations Course after Pre-Algebra?

Answers on P1EA, page 8.

ARITHMETIC REVIEW   Answers: [ ]'s

1. What kind of numbers will we deal with in the Foundation Course?   [**Real Numbers**]

2. What are Integers?   [**Whole or counting numbers both positive and negative**]

3. What are Rational Numbers?   [**Fractions, a/b where a and b are integers, b ≠ 0**]

4. What number is 3x100 + 2x10 + 7 + 0.4 + 0.05?   [**327.45**]

5. What do the Real Numbers correspond to?   [**Points on a straight line**]

6. What are the four basic operations?   [**+, -, x, ÷**]

7. What calculator will we use in the Foundation Course?

    [**TI-30Xa**]

8. What other three subjects will we learn about in the Foundations Course after Pre-Algebra?

    [**Algebra, Geometry, Trigonometry**]

Take the Quiz

P2 LESSON: THE NUMBER LINE, NEGATIVE NUMBERS

The Real Numbers we will be using in this Foundation Course can be corresponded to the points on a straight line called the Number Line.

We select a point to call Zero, 0.

We then select a point to the right of 0 and label it 1.

This establishes a "scale" and all numbers now correspond to one unique point on the line. (See below)

Positive numbers are to the right of 0, and Negative numbers are to the left of 0. The Negatives are a sort of "mirror" image of the Positives.

> a < b means a is to the left of b on the number line.
> a > b means a is to the right of b on the number line.
> a = b means a and b correspond to the same point.

You should be able to find the appropriate point on the line for any number, and vice versa.

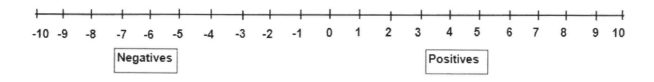

THE NUMBER LINE, NEGATIVE NUMBERS

1. Which letter is above 5.5?

2. Which letter is above 3?

3. Which letter is above -7?

4. Which letter is above -2.5?

5. What number is C above?

6. What number is L above?

7. What number is G above?

8. Is -3 > -6?

9. Is -3 < 1?

10. Is -6 > 0?

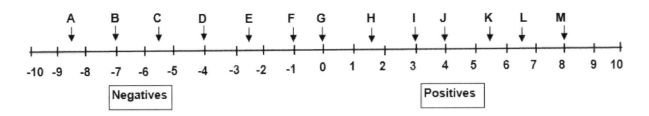

Problem: Given a number, find its location on the number line.
Problem: Give a point on the number line, estimate its value.

THE NUMBER LINE, NEGATIVE NUMBERS

Answers: [ ]'s

1. Which letter is above 5.5? [K]

2. Which letter is above 3? [I]

3. Which letter is above -7? [B]

4. Which letter is above -2.5? [E]

5. What number is C above? [-5.5]

6. What number is L above? [6.5]

7. What number is G above? [0]

8. Is -3 > -6? [Yes]

9. Is -3 < 1? [Yes]

10. Is -6 > 0? [No]

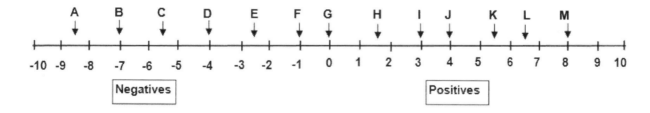

Problem: Given a number, find its location on the number line.
Problem: Give a point on the number line, estimate its value.

THE NUMBER LINE, NEGATIVE NUMBERS

1. Which letter is above -4?

2. Which letter is above 1.6?

3. Which letter is above -5.5?

4. Which letter is above 6.5?

5. What number is E above?

6. What number is K above?

7. What number is C above?

8. Is -1 > -3?

9. Is -3 < -1?

10. Is -6 > -7?

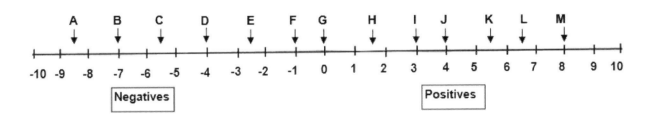

Problem: Given a number, find its location on the number line.
Problem: Give a point on the number line, estimate its value.

THE NUMBER LINE, NEGATIVE NUMBERS

Answers: [ ]'s

1. Which letter is above -4?   [D]

2. Which letter is above 1.6?   [H]

3. Which letter is above -5.5?   [C]

4. Which letter is above 6.5?   [L]

5. What number is E above?   [-2.5]

6. What number is K above?   [5.5]

7. What number is C above?   [-5.5]

8. Is -1 > -3?   [Yes]

9. Is -3 < -1?   [Yes]

10. Is -6 > -7?   [Yes]

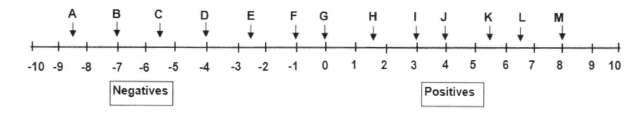

Problem: Given a number, find its location on the number line.
Problem: Give a point on the number line, estimate its value.

Revised 2023-03-31

P3 LESSON: RULES OF ADDITION   +   -

Rules of Addition: a, b, c represent an arbitrary real numbers

1. $a + 0 = a$ $7 + 0 = 7$

2. $a + b = b + a$ $15 + 6 = 6 + 15 = 21$

3. $(a + b) + c = a + (b + c)$ $(4 + 7) + 5 = 4 + (7 + 5) = 16$

4. $-(-a) = +a = a$ $-(-8) = 8$

5. $b - a = b + (-a)$ $7 - 3 = 7 + (-3) = 4$ $4 - 9 = 4 + (-9) = -5$

6. $a - a = a + (-a) = 0$ $8 - 8 = 0 = 8 + (-8)$

Note how addition works on the Number Line. Watch the video lesson that accompanies this lesson.

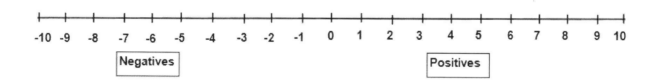

Problem: Given two numbers, find their sum's location on the number line.

Problem: Given two numbers, find their difference's location on the number line.

RULES OF ADDITION + -

1. 3 + 9 = ?

2. 126 + 879 + 438 = ?

3. 15.4 + 85.9 + 34.7 = ?

4. 56.4 - 87.2 = ?

5. 0.078 + 0.048 = ?

6. 87 - 341 = ?

7. 98 - (-34) = ?

8. Where is D + I on the number line?

9. Where is K - H on the number line?

10. -17.2 - 34.8 + 12.5 = ?

11. 245,400 + 782,900 = ?

12. -(-34) -(-23) = ?

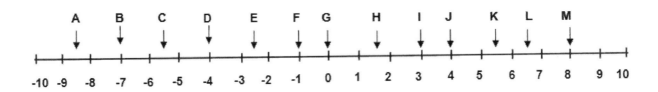

RULES OF ADDITION + -   Answers: [ ]'s

1. 3 + 9 = ?   [12]

2. 126 + 879 + 438 = ?   [1,443]

3. 15.4 + 85.9 + 34.7 = ?   [136.0]

4. 56.4 - 87.2 = ?   [-30.8]

5. 0.078 + 0.048 = ?   [0.126]

6. 87 - 341 = ?   [-254]

7. 98 - (-34) = ?   [132]

8. Where is D + I on the number line?   [F]

9. Where is K - H on the number line?   [J]

10. -17.2 - 34.8 + 12.5 = ?   [-39.5]

11. 245,400 + 782,900 = ?   [1,028,300]

12. -(-34) -(-23) = ?   [57]

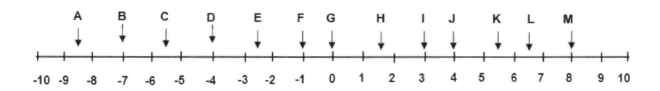

RULES OF ADDITION +, -

1. 13 + 29 = ?

2. 176 + 839 + 538 = ?

3. 17.4 + 35.3 + 34.9 = ?

4. 57.4 - 89.2 = ?

5. 0.068 + 0.036 = ?

6. 83 - 345 = ?

7. 92 - (-34) = ?

8. Where is J + F on the number line?

9. Where is K - F on the number line?

10. Where is 7.7 - 2.2 on the number line?

11. -(-37) + (-23) = ?

12. -(-37) -(-23) = ?

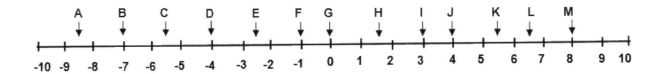

Take Quiz or review

RULES OF ADDITION +, -   Answers: [ ]'s

1. 13 +29 = ?   [42]

2. 176 + 839 +538 = ?   [1,553]

3. 17.4 + 35.3 + 34.9 = ?   [87.6]

4. 57.4 - 89.2 = ?   [-31.8]

5. 0.068 + 0.036 = ?   [0.104]

6. 83 - 345 = ?   [-262]

7. 92 - (-34) = ?   [126]

8. Where is J + F on the number line?   [I]

9. Where is K - F on the number line?   [L]

10. Where is 7.7 - 2.2 on the number line?   [K]

11. -(-37) + (-23) = ?   [14]

12. -(-37) -(-23) = ?   [60]

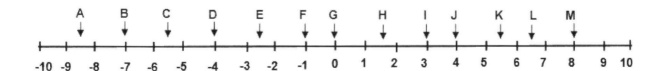

Take Quiz or review

P4 LESSON: RULES OF MULTIPLICATION X ÷

Multiplication of Real Numbers   axb or ab or a·b

a, b, c represents arbitrary real numbers

1. $a \times 0 = 0$ $7 \times 0 = 0$

2. $a \times 1 = a$ $13 \times 1 = 13$

3. $a \times b = b \times a$ [ab = bc] $15 \times 6 = 6 \times 15 = 90$

4. $(ab)c = a(bc)$ $(4 \times 7) \times 5 = 4 \times (7 \times 5) = 140$

5. $(-a) \times b = -(a \times b)$ $(-13) \times 12 = -156$

6. $(-a) \times (-b) = a \times b$ $-5 \times (-6) = 30$

7. $a \times (1/a) = 1$ $(a \neq 0)$ $7 \times (1/7) = 1$

8. $a \div b = a \times (1/b)$ $(b \neq 0)$ $12 \div 4 = 3 = 12 \times (1/4)$

Note how multiplication works on the number line. Watch the video lesson that accompanies this lesson.

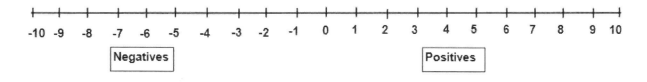

Problem: Given two numbers, find their product's location on the number line.

Problem: Given a number, find its reciprocal location on the number line.

RULES OF MULTIPLICATION   X   ÷

Multiplication of Real Numbers   axb or ab or a·b

1.   4 x 5 = ?

2.   12.4 x 13.8 = ?

3.   739 x 546 = ?

4.   3.2 x 7.8 x 5.4 = ?

5.   -34 x 27 = ?

6.   0.0034 x 0.056 = ?

7.   -87 x (-23) = ?

8.   Where is J x F on the number line?

9.   43.5 ÷ 6.9 = ?

10. 198 ÷ 5,748 = ?

11. 78 ÷ (-0.03) = ?

12. -45 ÷ -2.3 = ?

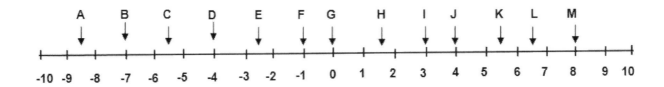

RULES OF MULTIPLICATION X ÷   Answers: [ ]'s

Multiplication of Real Numbers   axb or ab or a·b

1. 4 x 5 = ?   [20]

2. 12.4 x 13.8 = ?   [171.1]

3. 739 x 546 = ?   [403,494]

4. 3.2 x 7.8 x 5.4 = ?   [134.8]

5. -34 x 27 = ?   [-918]

6. 0.0034 x 0.056 = ?   [0.00019]

7. -87 x (-23) = ?   [2,001]

8. Where is J x F on the number line?   [D]

9. 43.5 ÷ 6.9 = ?   [6.3]

10. 198 ÷ 5,748 = ?   [0.034]

11. 78 ÷ (-0.03) = ?   [-2,600]

12. -45 ÷ -2.3 = ?   [19.6]

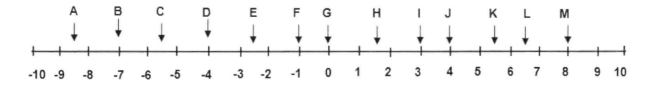

Take the Quiz or do more exercises on P4ES

RULES OF MULTIPLICATION   X   ÷

Multiplication of Real Numbers   axb or ab or a·b

1. 0.4 x 0.5 = ?

2. 17.4 x 54.8 = ?

3. -0.4 x 0.5 = ?

4. 3.4 x 7.8 x 5.7 = ?

5. -0.4 x (-0.5) = ?

6. 0.0037 x 0.046 = ?

7. 2 2/3 x 1 1/4 = ?

8. Where is -0.5 x 8 on the number line?

9. 4 3/5 ÷ 2 3/5 = ?

10. 0.198 ÷ 0.058 = ?

11. 78 ÷ (-0.3) = ?

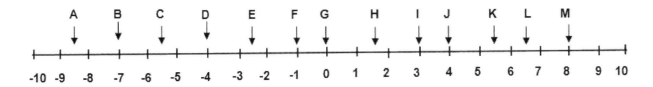

RULES OF MULTIPLICATION   X   ÷   Answers: [ ]'s

Multiplication of Real Numbers   axb or ab or a·b

1. 0.4 x 0.5 = ?   [0.2]

2. 17.4 x 54.8 = ?   [953.5]

3. -0.4 x 0.5 = ?   [-0.2]

4. 3.4 x 7.8 x 5.7 = ?   [151.2]

5. -0.4 x (-0.5) = ?   [0.2]

6. 0.0037 x 0.046 = ?   [0.00017]

7. 2 2/3 x 1 1/4 = ?   [3 1/3 = 10/3 = 3.3]

8. Where is -0.5 x 8 on the number line? [D]

9. 4 3/5 ÷ 2 3/5 = ?   [1 10/13 = 23/13 = 1.77]

10. 0.198 ÷ 0.058 = ?   [3.41]

11. 78 ÷ (-0.3) = ?   [-260]

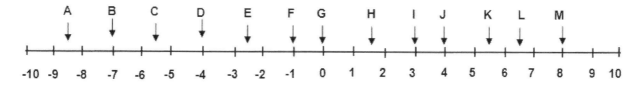

Take Quiz or review

Distributive Law and Factoring Real Numbers

a, b, c represents arbitrary real numbers

1. $ax(b + c) = axb + axc$ or $a(b + c) = ab + ac$ Simplifying

2. $axb + axc = ax(b + c)$ or $ab + ac = a(b + c)$ Factoring

x, y, z represent arbitrary numbers

3. $(x + y)z = xz + yz$ Simplifying

4. $xz + yz = (x + y)z = z(x + y)$ Factoring

Note how the Distributive Law works on the Number Line. Watch the Video lesson that accompanies this lesson.

DISTRIBUTIVE LAW   +   AND   X   COMBINED

Distributive Law and Factoring Real Numbers

1. $12x(34 + 23) = ?$

2. $(2.5 - 3.7)x6.9 = ?$

3. $(78.9 + 43.7)x(34.1 + 13.4) = ?$

4. $45x67 + 45x82 = 45x(?)$

5. $576x4 - 576x3 = ?$

6. $ab + ad = ax(?)$

7. $tu + vt = t(?)$

8. $ab^2 - ac^2 = ?x(b^2 - c^2)$

9. $5.4x2 + 5.4x3 + 5.4x4 + 5.4x5 + 5.4x6 = ?$

10. $z^3v + t^2v = (?)v$

11. $-3.4x(7.8 - 9.4) = ?$

12. $(123 + 876 - 276)x0 = ?$

13. $54.5(21.4 + 87.3 - 17.4)$

14. $0.02x(0.003 + 0.015) = ?$

15. $-17x(-6 - 9) = ?$

DISTRIBUTIVE LAW + AND X COMBINED
Answers: [ ]'s

Distributive Law and Factoring Real Numbers

1. $12x(34 + 23) = ?$ [684]
2. $(2.5 - 3.7)x6.9 = ?$ [-8.28]
3. $(78.9 + 43.7)x(34.1 + 13.4) = ?$ [5,823.5]
4. $45x67 + 45x82 = 45x(?)$ [67 + 82 = 149]
5. $576x4 - 576x3 = ?$ [576x(4-3) = 576]
6. $ab + ad = ax(?)$ [(b + d)]
7. $tu + vt = t(?)$ [(u + v)]
8. $ab^2 - ac^2 = ?x(b^2 - c^2)$ [a]
9. $5.4x2 + 5.4x3 + 5.4x4 + 5.4x5 + 5.4x6 = ?$ [5.4x20 = 108]
10. $z^3v + t^2v = (?)v$ [$z^3 + t^2$]
11. $-3.4x(7.8 - 9.4) = ?$ [5.4]
12. $(123 + 876 - 276)x0 = ?$ [0]
13. $54.5(21.4 + 87.3 - 17.4)$ [4,975.9]
14. $0.02x(0.003 + 0.015) = ?$ [0.00036]
15. $-17x(-6 - 9) = ?$ [255]

Take Quiz or do more exercises on P5ES

DISTRIBUTIVE LAW + AND X COMBINED

Distributive Law and Factoring

1. $13x(35 + 43) = ?$

2. $(3.5 - 4.9)x6.2 = ?$

3. $(7.9 + 43.7)x(4.1 + 13.4) = ?$

4. $42x69 + 42x82 = 42x(?)$

5. $579x7 - 579x6 = ?$

6. $as + ad = ax(?)$

7. $ta + bt = t(?)$

8. $ab^3 - abc^2 = ?x(b^2 - c^2)$

9. $abc - ac = acx?$

10. $z^2v - vt^2 = (?)v$

11. $(3 \frac{3}{4}) x (7/8 - 9/4) = ?$

12. $(12.3 + 886 - 276)x0 = ?$

13. $56.5(27.4 + 7.3 - 17.4) = ?$

14. $0.01x(0.008 + 0.015) = ?$

DISTRIBUTIVE LAW + AND X COMBINED

Answers: [ ]'s

Distributive Law and Factoring

1. $13x(35 + 43) = ?$ [1014]
2. $(3.5 - 4.9)x6.2 = ?$ [-8.7]
3. $(7.9 + 43.7)x(4.1 + 13.4) = ?$ [903]
4. $42x69 + 42x82 = 42x(?)$ [69 + 82 = 151]
5. $579x7 - 579x6 = ?$ [579]
6. $as + ad = ax(?)$ [(s + d)]
7. $ta + bt = t(?)$ [(a + b)]
8. $ab^3 - abc^2 = ?x(b^2 - c^2)$ [ab]
9. $abc - ac = acx?$ [(b - 1)]
10. $z^2v - vt^2 = (?)v$ [$z^2 - t^2$]
11. $(3 ¾) x (7/8 - 9/4) = ?$ [-5 5/32 = -165/32 = -5.16]
12. $(12.3 + 886 - 276)x0 = ?$ [0]
13. $56.5(27.4 + 7.3 - 17.4) = ?$ [977.5]
14. $0.01x(0.008 + 0.015) = ?$ [0.00023]

Take Quiz or review

P6 LESSON: FRACTIONS, A/B AND C/D, RULES

Rules for adding and multiplying and dividing fractions

a, b, c, d represent arbitrary real numbers with b ≠ 0, d ≠ 0

1. a/b + c/d = (ad + bc)/bd

2. a/b - c/d = (ad - bc)/bd

3. (a/b)x(c/d) = (ac)/(bd)

4. (a/b) ÷ (c/d) = (a/b)x(d/c) = (ad)/(bc), now c ≠ 0 also

5. Rules regarding - same as in multiplication. - ÷ - = +

You may learn to do this manually, or you can learn to use the TI-30Xa calculator. It does restrict denominators to be less than 1000.

****

Review the calculator lessons C10, C11, and C12, if necessary.

Work problems along with Dr. Del as he does them:

2/3 + 3/4 = 17/12 = 1 5/12

(-1/2) (x 2/3) = -1/3

(-1/2)x(-2/3) = 1/3

(3/4) + (7/8) = 1 5/8 = 13/8 = 1.625

FRACTIONS, A/B AND C/D, RULES

1. 2/3 + 3/4 = ?

2. 5 6/7 + 3 8/9 = ?

3. 1 7/8 − 1 1/2 = ?

4. 7/8 - 3/5 = ?

5. 6/7 x 3/8 = ?

6. 6/7 ÷ 3/8 = ?

7. Express 18/5 as a mixed fraction.

8. Express 18/5 in decimal form.

9. Express 0.35 as a fraction.

10. Express 4 7/8 as an improper fraction.

11. Express 4 7/8 as a decimal.

12. 3/4x(1 2/3 + 2 1/2) = ?

13. 2 3/4 − 2 3/8 = ?

14. 3 5/8 x 3 5/8 = ?

15. Express 2/3 as a decimal Real Number.

16. 1/a + 1/b = ?

FRACTIONS, A/B AND C/D, RULES   Answers: [ ]'s

1. $2/3 + 3/4 = ?$ [1 5/12 = 17/12 = 1.42]

2. $5\ 6/7 + 3\ 8/9 = ?$ [9 47/63 = 9.75]

3. $1\ 7/8 - 1\ 1/2 = ?$ [3/8]

4. $7/8 - 3/5 = ?$ [11/40]

5. $6/7 \times 3/8 = ?$ [9/28]

6. $6/7 \div 3/8 = ?$ [2 2/7 = 16/7 = 2.29]

7. Express 18/5 as a mixed fraction.   [3 3/5]

8. Express 18/5 in decimal form.   [3.6]

9. Express 0.35 as a fraction.   [7/20]

10. Express 4 7/8 as an improper fraction.   [39/8]

11. Express 4 7/8 as a decimal.   [4.875]

12. $3/4 \times (1\ 2/3 + 2\ 1/2) = ?$ [3 1/8 = 25/8 = 3.125]

13. $2\ 3/4 - 2\ 3/8 = ?$ [3/8]

14. $3\ 5/8 \times 3\ 5/8 = ?$ [13 9/64 = 13.14]

15. Express 2/3 as a decimal Real Number. [0.6667]

16. $1/a + 1/b = ?$ [(a + b)/ab]

Take Quiz or do more exercises on P6ES

FRACTIONS, A/B AND C/D, RULES

1. $2/5 + 3/8 = ?$

2. $2\ 6/7 + 1\ 2/3 = ?$

3. $1\ 5/6 - 1\ 1/2 = ?$

4. $5/8 - 4/5 = ?$

5. $4/7 \times 5/8 = ?$

6. $4/7 \div 5/8 = ?$

7. Express 19/7 as a mixed fraction.

8. Express 18/5 in decimal form.

9. Express 0.22 as a fraction.

10. Express $3\ 5/9$ as an improper fraction.

11. Express $3\ 5/9$ as a decimal.

12. $3/4 \times (2\ 2/3 + 3\ 1/2) = ?$

13. $2\ 3/5 - 2\ 3/4 = ?$

14. $(3\ 5/8)^2 = ?$

15. $1/ab + 1/cb = ?$

FRACTIONS, A/B AND C/D, RULES   Answers: [ ]'s

1. $2/5 + 3/8 = ?$ [31/40]

2. $2 \, 6/7 + 1 \, 2/3 = ?$ [4 11/21 = 95/21 = 4.5]

3. $1 \, 5/6 - 1 \, 1/2 = ?$ [1/3]

4. $5/8 - 4/5 = ?$ [-7/40]

5. $4/7 \times 5/8 = ?$ [5/14]

6. $4/7 \div 5/8 = ?$ [32/35]

7. Express 19/7 as a mixed fraction.   [2 5/7]

8. Express 18/5 in decimal form.   [3.6]

9. Express 0.22 as a fraction.   [11/50]

10. Express 3 5/9 as an improper fraction.   [32/9]

11. Express 3 5/9 as a decimal.   [3.56]

12. $3/4 \times (2 \, 2/3 + 3 \, 1/2) = ?$ [4 5/8 = 37/8 = 4.625]

13. $2 \, 3/5 - 2 \, 3/4 = ?$ [-3/20 = -0.15]

14. $(3 \, 5/8)^2 = ?$ [13 9/64 = 841/64 = 13.1]

15. $1/ab + 1/cb = ?$ [(c + a)/(abc)]

Take Quiz or review

P7 LESSON: SQUARES x^2 X SQUARED

$A^2 = A\text{x}A$ and we say: A squared

1. $(AB)^2 = A^2B^2$ Commutative Law yields this.

2. $(1/A)^2 = 1/A^2$

3. $(A + B)^2 = A^2 + 2AB + B^2$ Distributive Law yields this.

4. $(A - B)^2 = A^2 - 2AB + B^2$ Distributive Law again.

The x^2 Key will automatically square any number.

Work problems along with Dr. Del as you watch the video:

$(3\text{x}4)^2 = 144 = 3^2\text{x}4^2$ or $(3\text{x}4)\text{\textasciicircum}2 = 144 = (3\text{\textasciicircum}2) \text{ x } (4\text{\textasciicircum}2)$

$$(1/7)^2 = 1/7^2$$

$$(25.3)^2 = (25.3)\text{\textasciicircum}2 = 640.09$$

$$(-8)^2 = (-8)\text{\textasciicircum}2 = 64$$

$$A^2 > 0 \quad A^2 \text{ is positive, if A is non zero}$$

SQUARES X^2 X SQUARED

1. $(34.5)^2 = ?$

2. $(87)^2 = ?$

3. $(-23)^2 = ?$

4. $(2.4^2 + 3.5^2)^2 = ?$

5. $(65.9)^2 = ?$

6. $(89 + 57 - 32)^2 = ?$

7. $(12.3)^2/7.6$

8. $(15.4 \div 0.35)^2 = ?$

9. $(1 + 0.08)^2 = ?$

10. $(X + Y)^2 - X^2 - Y^2 = ?$

11. $(A - B)^2 - A^2 - B^2 = ?$

12. $(3/4)^2 = ?$

13. $3^2 + 4^2 = ?$

14. $(0.25)^2 = ?$

SQUARES x^2 X SQUARED   Answers: [ ]'s

1. $(34.5)^2 = ?$ [1,190.25]

2. $(87)^2 = ?$ [7,569]

3. $(-23)^2 = ?$ [529]

4. $(2.4^2 + 3.5^2)^2 = ?$ [324.36]

5. $(65.9)^2 = ?$ [4,342.81]

6. $(89 + 57 - 32)^2 = ?$ [12,996]

7. $(12.3)^2/7.6$ [19.91]

8. $(15.4 \div 0.35)^2 = ?$ [1,936]

9. $(1 + 0.08)^2 = ?$ [1.166]

10. $(X + Y)^2 - X^2 - Y^2 = ?$ [2XY]

11. $(A - B)^2 - A^2 - B^2 = ?$ [-2AB]

12. $(3/4)^2 = ?$ [9/16 = 0.5625]

13. $3^2 + 4^2 = ?$ [25 = 5^2]

14. $(0.25)^2 = ?$ [0.0625]

Take Quiz or do more exercises on P7ES.

SQUARES X^2 X SQUARED

1. $(3\ 4/5)^2 = ?$

2. $(8.7)^2 = ?$

3. $(-2/3)^2 = ?$

4. $(1.4^2 + 2.5^2)^2 = ?$

5. $(1\ 2/3 - 2\ 3/4)^2 = ?$

6. $(8.9 + 5.7 - 3.2)^2 = ?$

7. $(3.3)^2/(2.6)^2 = ?$

8. $(12.4 \div 0.85)^2 = ?$

9. $[(1 + 0.05)^2]^2 = ?$

10. $(X + Y)^2 = ?$

11. $(0.01)^2 = ?$

12. $(2/3)^2 = ?$

13. $1^2 + 2^2 + 3^2 + 4^2 + 5^2 = ?$

14. $(1.25)^2 = ?$

SQUARES X^2 X SQUARED   Answers: [ ]'s

1. $(3\ 4/5)^2 = ?$ [14.44 = 14 11/25]

2. $(8.7)^2 = ?$ [75.69]

3. $(-2/3)^2 = ?$ [0.444 = 4/9]

4. $(1.4^2 + 2.5^2)^2 = ?$ [67.4]

5. $(1\ 2/3 - 2\ 3/4)^2 = ?$ [1.17 = 1 25/144]

6. $(8.9 + 5.7 - 3.2)^2 = ?$ [1129.96]

7. $(3.3)^2/(2.6)^2 = ?$ [1.61]

8. $(12.4 \div 0.85)^2 = ?$ [212.82]

9. $[(1 + 0.05)^2]^2 = ?$ [1.22]

10. $(X + Y)^2 = ?$ $[X^2 + Y^2 + 2XY]$

11. $(0.01)^2 = ?$ [0.0001]

12. $(2/3)^2 = ?$ [4/9 = 0.444]

13. $1^2 + 2^2 + 3^2 + 4^2 + 5^2 = ?$ [55]

14. $(1.25)^2 = ?$ [1.56]

Take Quiz or review

P8 LESSON: SQUARE ROOTS $\sqrt{X}$

$\sqrt{A}$ is a number whose square will equal A.

$(\sqrt{A})^2 = A$, $\sqrt{A}$ can be positive or negative

A must be positive or $\sqrt{A}$ will not be a real number.

The $\sqrt{x}$ Key will calculate the square root of any positive number and give you the positive square root.

$\sqrt{x}$ will return an Error message on the TI-30Xa if $x < 0$.

$\sqrt{a^2} = a$, $\sqrt{x}$ and x^2 are inverses, i.e., undo each other.

Note: $\sqrt{(a + b)} \neq \sqrt{a} + \sqrt{b}$

****

$\sqrt{9} = 3$ $(-3)^2 = 3^2 = 9$

$\sqrt{16} = 4$ $4^2 = 16$

$\sqrt{89} = 9.4$ Note: $(9.4)^2 = 88.36$

$\sqrt{2} = 1.414213562....$ "Irrational" Number Infinite non-repeating decimal

Irrational means NO fraction will equal $\sqrt{2}$

Fractions   a/b, where a, b are integers, are called "Rational numbers"

$\sqrt{-6}$ Error   "Complex Number"

$\sqrt{(12 + 54)} = 8.12$ where $\sqrt{12} + \sqrt{54} = 3.46 + 7.39 = 10.8$

    You DO IT!   Then "play with" the $\sqrt{}$ function, key.

SQUARE ROOTS √ X

1. $\sqrt{81} = ?$

2. $\sqrt{56.9} = ?$

3. $\sqrt{745,365} = ?$

4. $\sqrt{(87)^2} = ?$

5. $(\sqrt{95})^2 = ?$

6. $\sqrt{(9 + 16)} = ?$

7. $(1 + \sqrt{32})^2 = ?$

8. $\sqrt{0.25} = ?$

9. $\sqrt{0.0001} = ?$

10. $(\sqrt{16} + \sqrt{9})^2 = ?$

11. $\sqrt{(1/4} = ?$

12. $\sqrt{(1/2)} = ?$

13. $\sqrt{(9/16)} = ?$

14. $\sqrt{(-9)} = ?$

SQUARE ROOTS $\sqrt{X}$

Answers: [ ]'s

1. $\sqrt{81} = ?$ [9]

2. $\sqrt{56.9} = ?$ [7.54]

3. $\sqrt{745,365} = ?$ [863.35]

4. $\sqrt{(87)^2} = ?$ [87]

5. $(\sqrt{95})^2 = ?$ [95]

6. $\sqrt{(9 + 16)} = ?$ [5]

7. $(1 + \sqrt{32})^2 = ?$ [44.3]

8. $\sqrt{0.25} = ?$ [0.5]

9. $\sqrt{0.0001} = ?$ [0.01]

10. $(\sqrt{16} + \sqrt{9})^2 = ?$ [49]

11. $\sqrt{(1/4} = ?$ [1/2]

12. $\sqrt{(1/2)} = ?$ [0.707]

13. $\sqrt{(9/16)} = ?$ [3/4]

14. $\sqrt{(-9)} = ?$ [Error]

Take Quiz or do more exercises on P8ES.

SQUARE ROOTS √ X

1. $\sqrt{144} = ?$

2. $\sqrt{256} = ?$

3. $\sqrt{123,456} = ?$

4. $\sqrt{(67)^2} = ?$

5. $(\sqrt{67})^2 = ?$

6. $\sqrt{(3^2 + 4^2)} = ?$

7. $(\sqrt{23} + \sqrt{32})^2 = ?$

8. $\sqrt{0.1111} = ?$

9. $\sqrt{0.000001} = ?$

10. $\sqrt{0.00001} = ?$

11. $\sqrt{(1/25)} = ?$

12. $\sqrt{(1 + 3 + 5 + 7 + 9)} = ?$

13. $\sqrt{(1+3+5+7+9+11+13+15)} = ?$

14. Do you see a pattern in the last two problems?

SQUARE ROOTS   √ X   Answers: [ ]'s

1. $\sqrt{144}$ = ?   [12]

2. $\sqrt{256}$ = ?   [16]

3. $\sqrt{123,456}$ = ?   [351.36]

4. $\sqrt{(67)^2}$ = ?   [67]

5. $(\sqrt{67})^2$ = ?   [67]

6. $\sqrt{(3^2 + 4^2)}$ = ?   [$\sqrt{5^2}$ = 5]

7. $(\sqrt{23} + \sqrt{32})^2$ = ?   [109.26]

8. $\sqrt{0.1111}$ = ?   [0.3333]

9. $\sqrt{0.000001}$ = ?   [0.001]

10. $\sqrt{0.00001}$ = ?   [0.00316]

11. $\sqrt{(1/25)}$ = ?   [0.2 = 1/5]

12. $\sqrt{(1+ 3 +5 + 7 +9)}$ = ?   [5]

13. $\sqrt{(1+3+5+7+9+11+13+15)}$ = ?   [8]

14. Do you see a pattern in the last two problems?

Take Quiz or review

1. $1/x = 1 \div x$ $1/4 = 1 \div 4 = .25$

2. $1/(1/x) = x$ $1/x$ is its own inverse

3. $1/a + 1/b = (a + b)/ab$ see fractions

4. $(1/x)^2 = 1/x^2$ see rules of exponents (P10)

5. $1/\sqrt{x} = \sqrt{(1/x)}$ see rules of exponents (P10)

∗∗∗∗∗∗∗∗∗∗∗∗∗∗∗∗∗∗∗∗∗∗∗∗∗∗∗∗∗∗∗∗∗∗∗∗∗

1/0 is undefined   1/0 Error   Never divide by 0

1/1/4 = 4   1/x Key is its own inverse

$1/9 = .11111111111...$

$(1/3)^2 = 1/3^2 = 1/9 = .1111111111...$

$1/\sqrt{16} = 1/4 = \sqrt{(1/16)} = .25$

$\sqrt{.5} = .707$ and $.5 < .707$

RECIPROCAL   1/X,   X ≠ 0

1. 1/7 = ?

2. 1/25 = ?

3. 1/0.05 = ?

4. 1/(0.1 + 0.2) = ?

5. $(1/3.3)^2$ = ?

6. $1/(3.3)^2$ = ?

7. √(1/9) = ?

8. $1/\sqrt{(3^2 + 4^2)}$ = ?

9. 1/1/7

10. 1/0

11. 1/(a + b) = ?

12. 1/√9 = ?

13. 1/(√16 + √25)

14. $(1 + 1/10)^2$ = ?

15. What operation is its own inverse?

RECIPROCAL   1/X,   X ≠ 0   Answers: [ ]'s

1. $1/7 = ?$ [0.1429]

2. $1/25 = ?$ [0.04]

3. $1/0.05 = ?$ [20]

4. $1/(0.1 + 0.2) = ?$ [3.33]

5. $(1/3.3)^2 = ?$ [0.0918]

6. $1/(3.3)^2 = ?$ [0.0918]

7. $\sqrt{(1/9)} = ?$ [1/3]

8. $1/\sqrt{(3^2 + 4^2)} = ?$ [0.2]

9. $1/1/7$ [7]

10. $1/0$ [Error]

11. $1/(a + b) = ?$ [1/(a + b)]

12. $1/\sqrt{9} = ?$ [1/3]

13. $1/(\sqrt{16} + \sqrt{25})$ [0.111111111]

14. $(1 + 1/10)^2 = ?$ [1.21]

15. What operation is its own inverse? [1/x]

RECIPROCAL $1/X$, $X \neq 0$

1. $1/4 = ?$
2. $1/0.5 = ?$
3. $1/0.01 = ?$
4. $1/(0.3 + 0.4) = ?$
5. $(1/2.5)^2 = ?$
6. $1/(2.5)^2 = ?$
7. $\sqrt{(1/25)} = ?$
8. $1/(1 \ 2/3) = ?$
9. $1/1/(3.7) = ?$
10. $1/45^0 = ?$
11. $1/1/a) = ?$
12. $1/\sqrt{49} = ?$
13. $1/1/1/1/1/1/5$
14. $1/1/1/1/1/1/1/5 = ?$

RECIPROCAL 1/X, X ≠ 0 Answers: [ ]'s

1. $1/4 = ?$ [0.25]

2. $1/0.5 = ?$ [2]

3. $1/0.01 = ?$ [100]

4. $1/(0.3 + 0.4) = ?$ [1.43]

5. $(1/2.5)^2 = ?$ [0.16]

6. $1/(2.5)^2 = ?$ [0.16]

7. $\sqrt{(1/25)} = ?$ [0.2 = 1/5]

8. $1/(1\ 2/3) = ?$ [0.6 = 3/5]

9. $1/1/(3.7) = ?$ [3.7]

10. $1/45^0 = ?$ [1]

11. $1/1/a) = ?$ [a]

12. $1/\sqrt{49} = ?$ [1/7 = 0.143]

13. $1/1/1/1/1/1/5$ [5]

14. $1/1/1/1/1/1/1/5 = ?$ [0.2 = 1/5]

Take Quiz or review

P10 LESSON: EXPONENTS Y^X Y > 0, X CAN BE ANY NUMBER

Definitions $\quad A^0 = 1 \quad\quad$ y^x is sometimes used for y^x

1. $A^n = A \times A \times \ldots \times A$, n times when n positive integer
2. $A^{1/n}$ is number such that $(A^{1/n})^n = A$
3. $A^{-n} = 1/A^n \quad$ Negative exponents.
4. $A^{n/m} = (A^{1/m})^n \quad$ Exponents defined for any rational number.
5. A^X can be defined for any real number. A > 0.

Rules of Exponents

6. $A^{n + m} = A^n \times A^m$
7. $(A^n)^m = A^{nm}$

$$************************************$$

$y^x \quad$ y times itself x times, $\quad$ y is base, $\quad$ x is exponent or power

$3^4 = 81 : 4^3 = 64 : 2^3 = 8$

Name	Digital Base 2		Metric Base 10	
Kilo K	$2^{10} =$	1024	$10^3 = 1000$	Thousand
Mega M	$2^{20} =$	1048576	$10^6 = 1000000$	Million
Giga G	$2^{30} =$	11073741824	$10^9 = 1000000000$	Billion
Tera T	$2^{40} =$	You do it.	$10^{12} = 12$ Zeros	Trillion

$8^{1/3} = 2$ $\quad\quad\quad\quad\quad\quad\quad\quad (987)^{1/3} = 9.956$

$9^{-2} = .0123 = 1/9^2$ $\quad\quad\quad\quad\quad (16)^{-1/2} = .25 = 1/4$

$(81)^{-1/4} = .3333\ldots = 1/81^{1/4}$

$177{,}147 = 3^{11} = 3^{(4 + 7)} = 3^4 \times 3^7 = 81 \times 2187$

$9^3 = (3^2)^3 = 3^6 = 729$ $\quad\quad\quad\quad 5^{2.6} = 65.66$

EXPONENTS Y^X ; Y > 0, X ANY NUMBER

1. 2^8 = ?

2. 12^3 = ?

3. $(17.1)^4$ = ?

4. 10^9 = ?

5. $(1 + 0.06)^{20}$ = ?

6. $15^{2.7}$ = ?

7. $1/(0.5)^4$ = ?

8. $25^{1/2}$ = ?

9. $81^{1/4}$ = ?

10. 5^{-2} = ?

11. 2^{30} = ?

12. $1{,}000 \times (1.06)^{100}$ = ?

13. $1{,}000 \times (1.07)^{100}$ = ?

14. $26 \times (1 + 0.06)^{400}$ = ?

EXPONENTS Y^X ; Y > 0, X ANY NUMBER

Answers: [ ]'s

1. $2^8 = ?$ [256]

2. $12^3 = ?$ [1728]

3. $(17.1)^4 = ?$ [85,503.6]

4. $10^9 = ?$ [1,000,000,000]

5. $(1 + 0.06)^{20} = ?$ [3.21]

6. $15^{2.7} = ?$ [1,497.77]

7. $1/(0.5)^4 = ?$ [16]

8. $25^{1/2} = ?$ [5]

9. $81^{1/4} = ?$ [3]

10. $5^{-2} = ?$ [0.04 = 1/25]

11. $2^{30} = ?$ [1,073,741,824   1 GIG]

12. $1,000 \times (1.06)^{100} = ?$ [339,302.08]

13. $1,000 \times (1.07)^{100} = ?$ [867,716.33]

14. $26 \times (1 + 0.06)^{400} = ?$ [3.446×10^{11} = 344,600,000,000]

Take Quiz or do more exercises on P10ES.

EXPONENTS Y^X ; Y > 0, X ANY NUMBER

1. 2^{10} = ?

2. 2^{20} = ?

3. 2^{30} = ?

4. 10^3 = ?

5. 10^6 = ?

6. 10^9 = ?

7. $1/5^2$ = ?

8. 5^{-2} = ?

9. $1{,}281^{1/4}$ = ?

10. $(5.98)^4$ = ?

11. 2^{64} = ?

12. $(1.02)^{2,000}$ = ?

EXPONENTS Y^X ; Y > 0, X ANY NUMBER

Answers: [ ]'s

1. 2^{10} = ?   [1,024 = K]

2. 2^{20} = ?   [1,048,576 = M]

3. 2^{30} = ?   [1,073,741,824 = G]

4. 10^3 = ?   [1,000 = K]

5. 10^6 = ?   [1,000,000 = M]

6. 10^9 = ?   [1,000,000,000 = G]

7. $1/5^2$ = ?   [0.04]

8. 5^{-2} = ?   [0.04]

9. $1,281^{1/4}$ = ?   [5.98]

10. $(5.98)^4$ = ?   [1,279]

11. 2^{64} = ?   [1.845x10^{19}]

12. $(1.02)^{2,000}$ = ?   [159,000,000,000,000,000]

[$1 invested at time of Christ's birth earning 2% per year
  compounded would be more money than in the world today.
  1% would yield only 440 million.]

Take Quiz or review

Made in United States
Orlando, FL
10 June 2023

34012449R00089